Essays on Shakespeare

Essays on
Shakespeare

Robert B. Heilman

Northrop Frye

Harry Levin

J. V. Cunningham

Gunnar Boklund

Maynard Mack

Gerald W. Chapman, *Editor*

PRINCETON, NEW JERSEY
PRINCETON UNIVERSITY PRESS
1965

PREFACE

THE essays in this volume were first presented as lectures at the University of Denver during the spring of 1964. The departments of English and Theatre invited six scholar-critics, of singular distinction and plural approach, to say about Shakespeare whatever they might care to say on the occasion of his four-hundredth anniversary. We prescribed no limits and shadowed forth no design. These distinguished men were free to speak about "Shakespeare" as of a reverend abstraction, and they now find themselves juxtaposed in one book unaware of what each has said and unaware also of what I may say as introduction. No valuable criticism, we reasoned, much less a coherent book of criticism, is stage-managed from outside except by the wildest luck. It exfoliates from a vital self engaged with learning, and, like good poetry, is as much discovered as planned, given an occasion. Our intent was to assemble six distinguished minds on a distinguished occasion and to see what would happen. Graciously, each came, spoke, and departed, and we alone enjoyed the privilege of comparison, which now becomes a wider privilege.

The essays are printed here substantially as given; they thus retain the flavor of the spoken word. The order of presentation has been slightly, but very slightly, rearranged to ease consecutive reading. The first three essays, boldly allusive and thematic, sweep through the whole canon of plays (and much of Shakespearean criticism) in pursuit of principle. The last three, more tightly analytic, burrow for principle more or less in single plays—one comedy and two major tragedies. The opening essay, by Robert Heilman, enlarges criticism beyond perception of aesthetic fact to include the society of perceivers and the ruling norms of perception—the "role" of Shakespeare in that great endless play which is lived and half-invented by his audience. The second essay, by Northrop Frye, illuminates a subtle dialectic in the language of Shakespeare or, more accurately, in his "poetic thinking" with language. The next two essays, by Harry Levin and J. V. Cunningham, open learned, humorous windows upon Shakespeare in his workshop; totally different in approach, they concur in his conscious artistry. The essay by Gunnar Boklund reexamines the enigma of Hamlet, and so doing reasserts a classic principle of "judgment"—commonsense grasp of the moral qualities of action in both the creation and interpretation of drama. In the concluding essay Maynard Mack peers into the all-too-human abyss of Lear's world and explains why, of all Shakespearean plays, *Lear* speaks with such contemporary force.

We sought diversity, and we found it abundantly. Such indeed is the diversity of mid-twentieth century criticism itself, with its sense of historic abysses to be bridged by myth, artistry, or scholarship; its disturbing wealth and awareness of alternatives; and not less remarkable, its self-conscious care for present value. Every reader will judge for himself at what points the lecturers cohere or dissent, and no one will expect, or should expect, an easy agreement.

If I may be allowed one small directive comment to the reader—for which the lecturers are in no way to be held responsible—I will ask him to notice their quiet, steady concern for the contemporary and living. Perhaps on a centenary occasion one is more likely than at other times to reflect on relevance, to be more than usually conscious of the present and of a long history of interpretations crowding in upon whatever one will say. But there is still more to notice. Criticism strives toward a vantage from which all literature, contemporary and past, is equally visible, and though no critic ever quite reaches it, some critics come much closer than others. The critics in this book are established scholars of Shakespeare who have also advanced understanding of the twentieth century and its literature. We planned the selection so, and it was the only plan we had.

Since the date of his lecture Maynard Mack's essay

has been printed in *The Yale Review,* Vol. LIV, No. 2 (December 1964); and a substantial part of J. V. Cunningham's essay will appear in a forthcoming volume of the Laurel Shakespeare Series published by Dell Publishing Company. We are grateful to both publishers for their willingness to share publication. I would like also, personally, to thank R. Miriam Brokaw of Princeton University Press for her enthusiastic help and patient encouragement.

GERALD W. CHAPMAN

Denver, Colorado
March 1, 1965

Essays on Shakespeare

CONTENTS

The Role We Give
Shakespeare

BY ROBERT B. HEILMAN

WHAT do we do to celebrate Shakespeare's four-hundredth anniversary? Like all public occasions, this one may release a torrent of banalities from a heavy overcast of cloudy minds. One might reconcile himself to this fate by accepting the dictum of a prominent Shakespearean: that everything said about Shakespeare is so quickly choked out by other things said about Shakespeare that if it is to stay alive it has to be said over again every ten years. Hence, if one only said something old, he might still think of himself as a refreshing rain that helps bring some flower into bloom again. As another alternative, he might aspire to be a high wind of novelty, sweeping all down before him by daring new pronouncements. But even the electric-storm, outrageous last word might not save him from the fate of becoming, in the end, only the latest in a long line of polemic commentators abusing their predecessors and each other. If he fights off the lust to conquer the Shakespeare text, to get it down by new formulae in which his own sensibility triumphs over the artist—the eternal pitfall of critical pride—he may fall into the opposite trap, in which the apparent virtue of humility before the art work turns out to be only his own incapacity to deal with it. He undergoes the ceaseless struggle between the trite giver of praise and the laborious upsetter of tradition, between those counter-figures within modern man—the congenital idolater, and opposite him the watchful debunker that our age has inflicted on all our psyches.

One might try to flee the hard struggle by proposing to adopt no attitude at all, to shun praise and blame, to have done with iconolatry and iconoclasm, and to settle for iconography. He might simply approach Shakespeare "because he is there" (to paraphrase the famous words that the mountain-climber used of the mountain). He would then acquire a full supply of all known technical paraphernalia, and climb, and make descriptive notes, as best he could; he might even perish upon the drifted slopes of annotation. A quite different kind of person, one given to hypothesis and speculation, might ask what the climber would do if he did not have the mountain. What if there were no Shakespeare? Would we lavish all our Shakespearean labors and devotions upon Marlowe, or Webster, or Beaumont and Fletcher? Or sup-

pose we had in our possession all the eulogies of Shakespeare, but no surviving texts, or only a few frag-
ments? How would we imagine the actuality that lay
behind the praise and adulation? And at this point another kind of theorist, a gamesman in epistemology,
might interpose, "Do we who possess texts do any
better in imagining Shakespeare than we would if we
had no texts? Shakespeare 'is there' all right, but what
Shakespeare? Do we study his image, or make an image by our own study habits? Do we respect what is
created, or create by expecting?"

Here let us jump from prologue to action. It may
be serviceable to look at the expectations that we
bring to Shakespeare. Consciously or not, we do come
to him with expectations, and possibly we help to
form him by our expectations. Be that as it may—I am
not pressing the idealist position—the sum of our expectations may tell us something, if not exactly about
Shakespeare, at least about the nature of the transac-
tion when we read him, study him, or see him played.

ii

The first expectation that I will record may seem, at
first blush, somewhat naïve. It was expressed to me
forty years ago in a moving-picture theatre where I
was an usher; it was held by an older employee, uned-
ucated, but extremely well read. He operated the pro-
jecting machines, he was a power in his union, he was
ugly in face, fierce in unspectacled eye, and tough in
manner; so it did him no professional damage to read

what he wanted to. He was doing Shakespeare at the time, and he became almost obsessed with the fact that Shakespeare is full, not only of what we call the facts of life, but of *double-entendres;* that such words as "die" and "will" and "nothing" have other meanings. He had not expected this, and he took it out on me; I was a high-school senior on the way to college and willy-nilly was held responsible for books in general. One day he stopped me by pulling at one of the scores of buttons that adorned my uniform, pointed to his volume of Shakespeare, and said, with positive bitterness, as if he had been betrayed, "And they call this a classic." Now he was no prude and not even faintly genteel; he talked and lived a lusty life. Nor was he a fool. For the expectation to which he was giving voice—as I was not to know until long after—was that a classic presents a nobler truth than that of everyday life, that a classical Shakespeare must, in the words Aristotle used of tragedy, represent man as better than in actual life. A classic writer will not waste time in saying the easy things that any man, however dull, can say in club or pub or privy, or in jesting on common topics suited for a little man's small talk; his task is not earth-bound, but superhuman, and he must be at an awe-inspiring altitude throughout the working day. His business is not the facts of life, but something much greater than the facts of life. We now interpret the evidence differently from my operator, whose vehemence scared me; but his view we recognize as ancient and persistent, and, if we ignore the difficulties of applying it, sound enough.

A radically different expectation is implied in a comment by J. B. Priestley, who in a recent memoir alludes to the grousing of soldiers in World War I. He writes, "Perhaps it was the Irish in them that lifted their grumbling, which never stopped, to an Elizabethan height. The only remarks that I have heard that Shakespeare might have borrowed all came from private soldiers in that war." [1] Unlike my cinema man, Priestley thinks of Shakespeare as drawing on the ordinary, the unelevated, the earthy: representing men as they are. Yet note: what is implied is a special dimension—an intensity and imaginativeness which convert the ordinary into the extraordinary, extract elevation from the earth-bound itself. Hence the phrase "Elizabethan height." Whereas for my moviehouse colleague, Shakespeare as classic had to keep his feet off the ground, for Priestley, Shakespeare can work from the trenches below the surface. Yet the key term is "work from": mud holes and common clay will do if they are in some way transformed, their everyday grossness "lifted" into a rarer allotrope, carbon into diamond; a body revealing a soul, not by dissolving itself but by verbal art finding and revealing an essence that has power over us.

My third witness is a writer and intellectual, who not long ago gave me a joyous account of Shakespeare

[1] J. B. Priestley, *Margin Released* (New York, 1962), p. 91.

at home: the reading aloud and the acting of parts, by himself and—this should be at least a small climax—his eleven-year-old daughter. They had just been doing *Hamlet* and *The Taming of the Shrew*, obviously an inclusive diet. In my friend's glowing report of these private theatricals, several elements stood out: the simple pleasure of the business—fresh, lively, spontaneous; the unaffected relish of the passages of bold bawdry; the general accessibility of the texts, with little help from what the guardians of the treasure call "apparatus." Here we have another sense of Shakespeare: Shakespeare as the source of plain delight, Shakespeare as family entertainment, Shakespeare as the good book in which all matters have a part and give pleasure, and as an open book to all who are open to it. As family entertainment the book yields nothing to the canons of propriety that in the name of the family were later to afflict the novel. As a traditional text, it has a scent of the mysteries, and mysteries imply professional interpreters to guide the laity; yet this text can speak directly and privately to the attending heart.

The Shakespeare canon is quite another matter to my fourth commentator, a friend deep in Freud. He assured me recently that before too long Freudian critics would have mastered most of Shakespeare. Freudian criticism would have proved itself by taking the giant into camp, or, in another metaphor, would have become a god by swallowing the god whole. My point is not a history of successive divinities, nor the validity of Freudian criticism, but the position of

Shakespeare as a reality that must be reckoned with by causes, systems, theories, and perspectives that seek our allegiance. They must say, "We subsume him" or "We are congruent with him" or "He proves us." He is claimed for different varieties of Christian thought, and as a voice of paganism; as a man of tragic vision, and as a grim cynic; as a representative of different sexual natures; as a lover of flowers, and a hater of animality; as a pure theatrical entertainer, and as a philosopher in drama; as a universal artist, and as a spokesman for the views and attitudes of his own day. Every such judgment reveals the beliefs of the judge, who says, in effect, "God is on my side." The need to find an ally in Shakespeare is revealed in another way by a scholar who in private life is a liberal and who acknowledged to me, sadly, his fear that Shakespeare lacks true social consciousness. The claim that "Shakespeare is ours" is registered in a different way by the Baconians and other such private sleuths and vigilantes. Whereas for most of us the word "Shakespeare" may refer interchangeably to writings and writer, the inseparable parts of a single reality, the Baconians demand that the sacred writings must issue from a prophetic voice with credentials that they can stamp approved. A country boy without college degrees or social advantages, they think, will never do.

So much for the diverse expectations with which men approach Shakespeare. As Schiller put it in "Kant and His Interpreters," "One who is opulent offers legions of famishing beggars food. When the kings con-

struct, carters find plenty of work." [2] T. S. Eliot
remarks that Shakespeare and other great artists "have
all been called upon to dignify a dubious theory." [3]
The present issue, however, is not the dubiousness of
theories applied to Shakespeare, but the quality that
makes Shakespeare irresistible to theorists of diverse
and contradictory persuasions. That quality, surely, is
a wholeness or completeness which is the sum of innumerable parts, a comprehensive statement that is the
sum of innumerable themes. Completeness or compre-
hensiveness is desirable for its own sake—to possess, to
be at one with, to sense as the ultimate extension of
one's own world view. But the Shakespeare completeness appears graspable and possessable to many men at
odds with each other, because of the innumerableness
of the parts: these parts we may consider incomplete-
nesses, partial perspectives, and as such they corre-
spond to the imperfect (but not necessarily invalid)
modes of seeing and understanding practiced by imperfect (but not necessarily wrongheaded) interpreters and theorists of different camps. Each interpreter
sees some part of the whole that does, we may say,
mirror him, and he then proceeds to enlarge the
mirror until it becomes the work as a whole. This is
simply to say that the most comprehensive soul, to use
Dryden's term, does comprehend many other smaller
souls; and it is understandable that each of these,

[2] Walter Kaufman, *Twenty German Poets* (New York, 1962),
p. 45.
[3] In the Preface to Leone Vivante's *English Poetry* (Carbondale,
Illinois, 1963), p. v.

humanly intent on grandeur, should try to become the whole. Hence the distortings, the stretchings, the thinnings that each of us can detect in Shakespeare interpretations, at least in the work of other interpreters.

One of the defenders of the Shakespearean wholeness against the tendency to mistake parts for the whole, Leone Vivante, alludes particularly to the practice of modern psychology in letting some part seize preeminence. In Shakespeare, Vivante argues, "consciousness" is complete, final, self-evident, not a façade for more limited elements. Shakespeare "does not replace consciousness with the subconscious, the unconscious, the complexes, the instincts, the subliminal." Vivante calls Shakespeare a bulwark against the "philosophical barbarism" of forgetting "the essential and common characters of consciousness." As long as Shakespeare is read, Vivante insists, "it will be difficult for English-speaking people to forget the soul for the complexes, the instincts, the subconscious, the unconscious, and the tropisms." [4] Though one might want to qualify some of the details of this argument, still the spirit is right: it identifies a mechanical, gimmicky kind of criticism that is reductive because it lacks a sense of wholeness.

Suppose we amalgamate these comments that reveal different perspectives, definitions, and, as I called them originally, expectations. In sum, Shakespeare is above the ordinary, petty, mundane, vulgar level of speech

[4] *English Poetry,* pp. 59–60.

and thought; he represents a nobler, higher realm of being. Shakespeare has both feet on the ground; but in him the common ground is transfigured, revealed in a new dimension; nothing is too mean for him, but the mean itself is raised to a supernal plane. Shakespeare is the ultimate all-purpose book, with imaginative breadth and depth, for a humanity not limited by age or sex, immediately open to all who will read (a view not entirely shared by the caste of professional interpreters). But if read by all, it can be claimed by all. Radicals and traditionalists, utopians and cynics, philosophers of different schools and theatrical historians —all assert that he is their man; the counter-view, of course, is that he can claim all of them as constituents of his own being. He is the all-embracing artist, the ecumenical man, and hence more than man.

iii

What follows? I suggest that into the interplay between Shakespeare and ourselves there has come an element which may be described, not inaccurately, by the word "religious." (I will use the word to signify various matters—spiritual, historical, and institutional.) There are mysterious origins; there was a piercing new vision which suggests "revelation." There are sacred texts, not always entirely plain in meaning, but exacting high reverence from us. They tell perceptive tales of men as we know them, but also constitute a transcendent myth which arches over and supersedes all ordinary actualities. There is a priesthood of interpreters, an establishment of those who have the mysteries in their keeping. Yet the protestant spirit is always lively; new exegetes keep springing up, and old gospels are poured into new bottles. The ultimate protestantism of course is the belief in that private power, be it conscience or consciousness, to which the divine voice can speak directly, in defiance of all hierarchies, new and old.

The birth and death of the divine figure are not without mystery. Some years ago a visitor to Warwickshire concluded "that the whole intellect of Warwickshire had been exhausted in the production of one man, as since Shakespeare's day there had never been a native of the country who was not next door to an idiot." [5] If a thatched cottage is a little more ample than a manger, still it has enough lowliness to nurture myth. Not only has the tomb become a shrine, but there are those who insist that if opened it would be found empty. Whom seek ye? We have not only this primary shrine but many secondary ones; there are many cathedral towns with public worship at stated times. If seven cities claimed Homer dead, at least as many Stratfords claim dead Shakespeare as a live box-office attraction. He liveth. Indeed, a Stratford by any other name will smell as sweet to thronging tourists and will sweeten the pot as much for all who serve the faith. Pilgrims come from everywhere to these central shrines, where all kinds of relics, me-

---

[5] Janet Dunbar, *Mrs. G. B. S.: A Portrait* (New York, 1963), p. 45.

mentoes, and objects sacred by association are for sale, and hawkers labor around the clock. Every true faith always has a distribution problem and stimulates much business effort; shrines and commerce are paired in a complementary marriage. Original, primitive rites are practiced to solemnize the worship—communions of ancient food and drink, grave dances on the green within the cathedral close, concerts with what we might call Old Testament instruments. These perhaps stimulate the tithing spirit.

Not only here at the shrine, but everywhere, one may secure the sacred works in authorized texts, collaboratively prepared by different editorial septuagints. The works appear in a remarkable number of editions as scholars labor hard to put forth new versions of the scriptures—actuated, as they may be, by a passion for textual purity, by a simple desire to spread the truth, or by a sense of the emoluments that may attend greater editorial perfection. Some of these editions are light and easy to carry and are available to the masses at only nominal fees. Someday, I suspect, there will be a Gideon Shakespeare. The scriptures themselves are a sacred battlefield upon which scholars and critics may prove themselves and their faiths. These warriors may be specialists in *loci critici*, defenders of published theses, or antagonists in massive theological disputations. There is often a crusading spirit, a note of rescuing the sacred from the profane. Sometimes, however, the combatants seem to be speaking only to each other, playing theological war games at a great remove from the real affairs of the church. Still, with a moderate success here, a man may advance in the hierarchy to a cathedral position or chair. Then he must help fight off the new heresies that keep cropping up, to be beaten back or slowly transformed into new orthodoxies, as the true faith is expounded in a dozen different ways that are not always compatible. But fortunately the texts always survive; the biblia always remain open to all who will quest for either their pristine or their eternal substance.

The sanctuaries in which our public observances and rites are carried on have a recognizable similarity. Tradition survives even as one new architectural certainty replaces another, since all the edifices, whatever the latest vogue, provide for a focussing of the congregation upon the celebrants. Recently, indeed, tradition seems to have become stronger: more and more of our edifices strive to resemble the original primitive gathering-place of the faithful, one whose name has great symbolic value for a universal creed: the Globe. Along with this goes, in some of the shrine cities, a rejection of latter-day hedonistic supplements that may damage the true spirit of the rites. A deity called the "sweet swan of Avon" can hardly be worshiped indoors, and anachronistic roofs have sometimes been abandoned. For a long time the rites themselves had a special old-style ecclesiastical flavor: they seemed long-drawn-out, relentlessly complete, and very tiresome, but still congregations were dutiful, feeling that they had contact with some higher reality and that it had probably been good for them and made them better men. But in the shrine cities, things have changed: the rites have a new speed and zest presumed to renew the vitality of primitive days. We of the English-speaking world still adhere to the original tongue; so far I have heard of only one effort to render a text into our modern vulgate. Finally, we should remember the vast importance of ceremonial in our observations, especially those that have to do with anniversary occasions like the present one. A notable Shakespearean has suggested that we celebrate Shakespeare's four-hundredth only by trying to teach our classes better. Heresy! It is like proposing that we celebrate Christmas only by individually cultivating a charitable spirit in private life. It will not do. We crave public forms: even listening to a visiting evangelist.

In sum, we have texts that have a magical hold upon us; these are dramatized in public renderings at scheduled times and places, some of them famous for this alone. They are traditional; they unite past and present. They must find general support, and the central activity begets a dozen kinds of by-products and side-lines. In these notes on theatre as church do we have only a strained simile, a tour de force in analogy, good for some laughs but otherwise likely to bespeak only the ingenuity of the comparer? One better acknowledge that this is all there may be to it. Still it may be that the comparison does reveal something about the nature of our transactions with Shakespeare, and in the name of Shakespeare, particularly in our own times. In some quarters there is a disposition to believe that we have put religion behind us, that it belonged to a phase of consciousness now outgrown. There is an alternative view, however: that we do not have a choice between religion and no-religion, but only between one religion and another, or between, let us say, a deeper and a shallower one. In this regard, modern developments have pushed us into more choices than those faced by our ancestors for a good many centuries. We appear to have moved away from the old and in its place, or at least in competition with it, to have invented three new religions—the religion of science, the religion of humanity, and the religion of art. The religion of science gratifies our persisting love of miracles, and we have faith that it is a docile agent of the religion of humanity. The religion of humanity I will not linger on except to remark that, since it is naturally polytheistic, it begets a variety of political sects and social gospels that are alike only in placing the second coming of utopia much ahead of earlier and vaguer scheduling.

The religion of art is more esoteric: it exacts more, promises less, has a more monastic tinge, does not always do well in getting the pie out of the sky and in through the skylight, and in effect warns its postulants that they may end up fools rather than cardinals. Besides, the religion of art has a Luciferian tinge frightening to some hopefuls and excessively attractive to grade-B artists: the priest risks not only being an ass by failure but contemning God by success. Le Corbusier said: "What makes an artist, you see, are the moments when he feels that he is more than a man." [6] Ibsen's sculptor Rubek tells his wife, "Did I not promise to take you up with me to a high mountain and show you the glory of the world?" [7] Ibsen's master builder Solness talks back to God, climbs too high, and pitches into a deep hole in the earth.[8] Stephen Dedalus knows exactly whom he is quoting when he declares, "*Non serviam.* I will not serve." Such allusions, such images, thrive only in the felt kinship of art with religion.

But if for the broader term "art" we substitute the narrower term "poetry," we actually increase the range of this mode of religious experience. We have now not only a creative priesthood and its icons to admire casually but enduring texts to sustain the laity and to hold them in more than transitory attention. Keats almost instinctively thought of the poetic activity as religious.[9] Wordsworth and Shelley both held enthusiastically to this conception, and, as the nineteenth century went on, it "became a platitude" to impute to poetry the function once exercised by creeds now "shaky or crumbling." [10] W. K. Wimsatt

[6] Albert Camus, *Notebooks 1935–1942*, tr. Philip Thody (New York, 1963), p. 132.

[7] *When We Dead Awaken*, Act II.

[8] *The Master Builder*, Act III.

[9] W. J. Bate, *John Keats* (Cambridge, Massachusetts, 1963), pp. 136–37.

[10] Walter E. Houghton, *The Poetry of Clough* (New Haven and London, 1963), p. 13; cf. Houghton's *Victorian Frame of Mind* (New Haven, 1959), pp. 152ff.

sums up for our own day: ". . . we live in an age" that makes "momentous claims for poetry—claims the most momentous conceivable. . . ." [11] So much for this; I have wanted only to go far enough to show that there is no novelty in thinking of the poet as divinely creative and of poetry as having a religious function. We may then speak of the religious quality of the Shakespeare myth, and of our responses to it, without seeming to be trading on a contrived absurdity or plotting an outrage to trap the mind's eye.

i v

If we use this perspective, what do we see in Shakespeare? It may be the right question to ask about a man whose hold upon us has been increasing steadily for four centuries. For behind everything there is the seer or visionary; then there are the massive texts embodying more of reality than most ordinary men can encompass in a lifetime; and then the regular, year in and year out, public presentations that bring us together in decorous and ritualistic observances. Nominally all this has to do with "pleasure" and "entertainment," and one might claim no more for it than that it is entertainment of a high order. And it has to be that. Yet into our reception of the entertainment there enters something like reverence; it is not fashionable to make serious criticism of these dramas or this dramatist; if we are not always entertained, in fact, we are

[11] *What To Say About a Poem,* CEA Chapbook, ed. Donald Sears (1963), p. 19.

inclined to blame ourselves rather than the fare; for we feel that we have been in touch with something nobler than the theatre customarily affords, and that, if not always excited or titillated as we might be by, say, a night-club act, we are still in some way lifted, made greater, deepened by being here. Behind the entertainment, I surmise, we intuit a double revelation: a sharper definition of what we somewhat amorphously know from experience and then an unexperienced, perhaps unapprehended, perhaps unguessed-at reality that may always elude precise identification but is still for us an ultimate source of form and meaning.

But how do we receive this? How view it? Do we call it truth? Or do we profess to find codes or imperatives? Or do we seek betterment? Or consolation, or, more affirmatively, support? Or wholeness? Or do we experience a mystery which is an end in itself? Or a membership beyond that of mundane societies? I am trying here to introduce a set of representative terms that might be used by quite different kinds of people if they tried for a verbal assessment of what religious engagement implies. I mean to be descriptive, not normative. I want now to see how such terms might fare as we tried to accommodate them to our experience of Shakespeare.

Have we then been in touch with something that we might call truth? Perhaps. But it is an impression or feeling that it would be difficult to justify, to invest with a content that would be communicable to others. One might name a set of characters, from Iago to

Iachimo, from Falstaff to Caliban, from Hotspur to Prospero, that could be called "true." But they are not the instruments of propositions, nor authoritative voices through whom the plays speak; they are not prophets, mouthpieces for Shakespeare; what he says or thinks we do not know with certainty. It is possible to describe what the play "says"; but it is hard to reach a consensus even on that, and whatever consensus there is can change within a decade. The ceaseless conflict among interpreters, whatever master truth may be thought to lie just ahead of their farthest energetic probings, simply renders cloudy the supposition that sense of truth is the central experience of those who join the assemblage with special expectations and are in some way satisfied.

Yet whatever comes through has a validity that one would never deny. Would it come through as rule or mandate or set of injunctions? To ask this question is to answer it: that which only mistily serves the sense of truth will not do better for the sense of law. Richard III hardly strikes us as a commandment in the form of a horrible example; nor, in their different ways, do Iago and Coriolanus. Each of these, indeed, through charm or skill or courage may evoke, if not actual sympathy, at least a kind of undefined responsiveness that may unaccountably shade whatever thou-shalt-not may be read in their overt conduct. Antony has so much charm that what once was taken to be an erring life is now read as an escape from constraints upon aspiring humanity. Prince Hal and Falstaff and

Hotspur do not so much enjoin the whole man as speak seductively to different parts of him; and if Prince Hal seems to speak to the largest part, he now has many detractors to undermine his apparent authority.

If it seems a little naïve to deny what mature man would never affirm, still the sense of a directive character in great literature is not a monopoly of the unsophisticated. Men find it hard to divorce faith and ethics, sacred text and secular style, true knowing and right doing; communion with the superhuman, it naturally seems, should diminish the nonhuman, the subhuman, the inhuman. The religion of the humanities should make its saving mark upon humanity; Shakespeare should do some refining of human material, some ennobling of spirit. Surely an advocacy of him must imply some such profit. But a glimpse of those who have had most intimate contact with the master must cast some shadow upon the dream of beneficent influence. The professors of the humanities in general, or of Shakespeare in particular—those who have been in longest and closest touch with the great spirit—sometimes appear to have gained little. They may turn out to be little more than technicians, skilled in ancient usages, printing practices, obscure texts, and odd corners of history, and untouched by the civilizing spirit of the great creator. Instead of reach and urbanity of mind, scholars and critics may have developed pride of role, and taken on an arrogance as chilling as that of scientists presumably less subject to influences believed to modify rudeness of demeanor and feeling. As Henry Ryecroft came to recognize, "learning does not necessarily civilize, and . . . a man (may) remain a lettered barbarian." [12] If we turn to that other priesthood that interprets the divine Shakespeare to the laity, the theatre people, we may find a different vanity, prima donnas of both sexes, and a disposition to assorted kinds of perverse behavior. We should not intimate that these manifestations of egotism—the vanity or condescension of the university Shakespearean, or the self-indulgences of the theatre Shakespearean—are the rule. The point is simply that the guardianship of the mysteries does not guarantee largeness of mind or gentleness of bearing. If those closest to the source of values often remain untouched, we may wonder what hope there is for ordinary men who approach the sacred fount only now and then.

If these ordinary men do not find truth or governance or benign influence, what else may they come upon? Consolation or comfort or support? Hardly, at least in any obvious or immediate sense. The tragedies record profound catastrophes in the world and in the self; though they do come to rest on a note of moral recovery, this has a slenderness in which there is no easy assurance about the general tenor of life. If all ends well for Bertram and Helena, still it has required some extraordinary ingenuity and good fortune to

[12] Jacob Korg, *George Gissing* (Seattle, Washington, 1963), p. 242.

bring a chilly and selfish husband to the acceptance of his devoted wife. Vincentio, the Duke of Venice, has to be morally and psychologically omniscient, and superhumanly astute in practical affairs, to prevent his kingdom from falling into the moral depths opened up before us by the self-serving of Angelo and Claudio. The tardy abjuring of their feud by the Capulets and Montagues is slender compensation for the injuries sustained when the pursuit of family honor recognized no bounds. Hence one would be surprised to find in Shakespeare a note of blessedness to come, or of an ever-present help in trouble. There is indeed a subtle balance of the forces of damnation and salvation, as in the Christian vision, but this unillusioned picture of reality hardly affords the faithful the comforting sense of cosmic well-being sometimes apparently derived from religious experience.

If we use the word "support," however, we do name a way in which Shakespeare serves. It is the way of venerable texts whose authenticity has impressed itself on the human imagination: he has said many things in what seems an ultimate form, and he is a fountainhead of quotation and universal center of allusion. "A rose by any other name" comes to the mouth as readily as "Pride goeth before a fall," and seems no less wise. A quotable line is one that has shed its context and taken on independent life. Very significantly, Shakespeare scenes and character relationships have also taken on independent life and have provided basic formulations upon which other writers rely. The Ophelia-Laertes relationship is strongly felt near the end of Goethe's *Faust*, Part I, and the Hamlet-Gertrude-Claudius triangle echoes throughout Chekhov's *Sea Gull*. Lillo's *London Merchant* tries to echo *Macbeth*, and the modern musical *The Fantasticks* relies heavily on the Romeo-Juliet situation. When Horace Walpole was inventing the Gothic novel, and Scott the historical novel, both felt that they were extending Shakespeare, and Keats thought of Shakespeare as presiding over his own composition. Others draw on Shakespeare for such support because his characters and situations and formulations have that urgent, irrefutable quality that we call mythic; hence their presence affords a sense of spaciousness or wholeness. They become inviting and compelling, exactly like Biblical myths: we think easily of modern Job and Noah plays, of Satan figures in the novel, of the enlarging presence of the Cain and Adam motifs in Wilder's *Skin of Our Teeth* and Fry's *Sleep of Prisoners*.

V

When Shakespeare stories become mythical and are wound into modern plots, these are the more comprehensive; they offer wider realms in which we move closer to totality. We come, then, to another matter in which the function of Shakespeare texts has an affinity with the religious. We have a perennial problem of getting from a smaller to a larger sense of life. It is a human habit to be always, as we move from age to age, drifting into new constrictions; every new liberating perspective imposes its own rigidities; we flee from one half-truth through a wide-open door that turns out to lead us to another half-truth. We run from the excessive spirituality of the nineteenth century to the excessive physicality of the twentieth, from the hyper-genteel to the self-assured vulgar, from a strong sense of the unmentionable to the inability to stop mentioning it, from tiptoeing over the surface of life to being unable to get up to the surface from the substrata. We are always in flux, trying now this strait and now that. Fortunately there is help in a large and open body of literature such as the Shakespearean—a full sea of possibility. Some instinct for safety, an unconscious effort to remedy our own partialness, draws us to this sea. We do not articulate this, and we should not; it is simply that behind our devotion to the texts and our attendance at never-ending rites of presentation lies the faith that we are coming into a world of great breadth and depth, with insights and mandates different from our own, perhaps none of them better than our own but at least extending and supplementing them. We need not look long at some of Shakespeare's episodes and figures to imagine them in our own day, with a different style formed by a different world. With us, the storm in *Lear* would be an atmospheric disturbance due to a low-pressure area and rather frightening in insurance circles, not a symptom of cosmic disorder. The Capulets and Montagues, we suspect, would go underground, keep shooting it out for generations, and above all things refuse to say a word to the Duke or any other authority. Prospero would go to an enemy country, organize aid against his own, and become a tireless fomenter of civil broils, as well as a parent not likely to train up a Miranda. Ophelia would slap Hamlet's face or go out with some other courtier, Cordelia would talk back, and Desdemona would send for her lawyer. Macbeth would claim that Duncan had not worked for the best interests of the country, and on the throne Macbeth would seem so invincible that it would be years before his pragmatic miscalculations would put him in danger. Iago would be working for some fanatic organization at one extreme or another and whispering of betrayals to as large a public as would think him an honest man. Othello would have a spectacular trial in which his defense would be temporary insanity.

This translation must not be overdone, however, nor by a simple reversal of the old dogma of progress is it to be inferred that we are always the losers. But the analogies that I have drawn, if they are valid, should serve to sketch that other fullness of the Shakespeare world that I surmise we are drawn to and in some way rely on. For there may be an avenue to well-being in these cogent dramatic representations of ways of fidelity and of obligation, of devotion to justice, of sense of imperative—of these modes of forming the personality that may be valuable alternatives to the hasty self-assertion, or change of route, or disengagement ("I won't play"), the retaliation, the excuse, the justification, the racking of the law to escape from its grasp. We sense some unclear truth, perhaps, in doctrines of order and degree, concepts which on the face of it we seem to have outworn, and which yet conform to human habits that outlive the changes of public doctrine. In the concepts of chain of being and of nature we may find intimations of a unity more satisfying than that provided by our stringently naturalistic norms, and one whose possibilities extend our apprehension of reality. The doctrine of *pietas* might free us from some of the constrictions of the word "piety," whose main import, for us, is that devoutness is but a self-deception or a stratagem. We sense the need to escape from such bonds upon thought and feeling. The instinctive hope of escaping from the partial, and locating avenues to the whole, must find some encouragment in Shakespeare's characters; repeatedly they take us into a fullness which in our daily actuality we pare away into lesser and safer forms. In Imogen we contemplate a fullness of romantic charm that still does not make us soar over reality, in Claudius a powerful worldly drive that still is not freed from conscience and inner turmoil, in Emilia a passion for truth bitterly forced out of an easygoing worldliness, in Hotspur a destructive but by no means ignoble passion for an idea, in Goneril an ultimate of calculation paradoxically destroyed by lust, in Lady Macbeth a power-lust cheated by the exhausting rigors of calculation, in Cleopatra an ultimate of instinct that moves unerringly toward its ends, ready to triumph by snatching now life, now death. Through such characters we constantly transcend ordinary limits.

Perhaps we achieve another kind of transcendence, make another kind of move toward totality. Let us approach this by noting a final example of a Shakespeare character modernized: a Macbeth of our day would see no ghosts. How then do we, who see no ghosts, receive the apparition of the dead Banquo? Do we take the trouble to reassure ourselves that this is one man's ghost, a thickening of the air moulded by a deeply shadowed mind? Or take the ghost of the elder Hamlet: are we at pains to remind ourselves that this comes out of an older view of reality, a discarded physics? Or what do we do with the spirits of Gloucester's victims in *Richard III*, with the omens and soothsaying in *Julius Caesar*, with the vision of Posthumus in *Cymbeline*, with oracle and dream in *Winter's Tale?* Surely we do not trouble to dismiss these beings and these events as quaint relics of an antique science, not admissible in our own, but to be endured like an archaic accent and vocabulary translatable into some modern tone and idiom. How do we deal with the witches in *Macbeth*, those traffickers in the unseen or the not-yet-seen, prophets always corroborated by the event? To reject their literal character is to do damage to the deeply ironic plot of a man hurrying a destined rise that he does not quite trust, and fighting a destined fall in the erring trust that it is not due; to seek a symbolic character is to end up with nothing.

Even more so for Prospero's magical powers, which he first uses to good end and then abjures—a double moral process hardly to be dealt with as no more than amiable make-believe.

It is imaginable that in some way we accept these marvels—not merely by the naturalizing process to which we are prone, since it is not often applicable; nor by the symbolizing process, which must too much tax our inventiveness; nor by that gracious suspension of disbelief that permits the work to live at all. It is imaginable, rather, that we accept what in some obscure manner answers to something in us—to an inclination for, and a sense of, mystery that does not quite surrender to the commanding patterns of rationalistic life. Indeed, the more rational the ordering of existence, the greater the thirst for mystery; and our own is unslaked. Mostly we appease it in shoddy ways, by automation; and so we have readiness for the larger mystery that is not snuffed out by the mundanely factual in the last chapter of detective triumph. But even to be thus open to the unresolved may be sentimental indulgence. What justifies the sense of mystery is, in the end, that quality of the mysterious event that makes it seem, not a teasing and unresponsive puzzle, but a breaking-through of transcendental reality. Some such experience may be provided reputably by the spirits, the visions, all the strange existences and events beyond nature that Shakespeare keeps coming back to and setting forth for our contemplation. Through mystery, that is, we grasp a little more of the totality which we hazard is the felt essence of Shakespeare. And in reminder: mystery and totality are attributes of the reality ordinarily called religious.

Let me, in concluding, restate, alter the perspective, and make one addition. Shakespeare offers comprehensive, multiple modes of experience that we can denote by the word "community." One cannot use the term without risk. It may encourage self-consciousness in a realm where what is authentic has to be spontaneous; it may seem too grand; it may image something schmaltzy, that is, a cosy sort of fraternity where all conspires toward the insulated safety and ease of the individual. But the concept of community will not become sentimental if the shared experience has the breadth and depth implied when we speak of totality. The greater that which is held in common, the more exacting the participation; the myth of the transcendental enlarges that in which we hold membership, and demands a more onerous responsiveness. The simplest and most accessible manifestations of community are the ceremonial public gatherings in which all men may receive presented myths—myths that, antique as they are, still seem not simply evocative archaisms but live orderings of reality. Further, we possess the texts; they are a common possession, and we belong to each other by possessing them; but the common possession is a great one, and so our commonalty is a highly meaningful one. The ultimate body to which all may belong is the vision that infuses the dramas; it is not an easy one, and it cannot be so if its community is a true one. For there is such a thing as a pseudo-community. It is infected with idyllic utopianism; it formulates good and evil in simple topical propositions; it has rules for getting rid of what displeases virtuous man. Works of apparent art may foster a pseudo-community. If Shakespeare leaned in that direction, he would portray a world in which no Antony emerged to subvert the nobly intended subversion of ambitious Caesar; in which demagogic alertness and heroic rashness would not so quickly combine to defeat Coriolanus; in which Iagos, if they existed, would be sterilized before their destructive impulses had succeeded. Instead he makes us always aware of the circumstances that may conspire against the hopeful scheme; of the disasters that may be brought on by the personality in large part admirable; of our weakness before con men and men of malice. The community that he offers us costs much, and we may be obliged to be more adult than we expect. A whole series of comedies play for responses of which the simplest souls are capable, and then suddenly demand a grown-up intelligence of which gags and gimmicks give no warning. *The Comedy of Errors* promises us free laughs at mechanical men, but some of these begin to think and feel, and our belly laughs are out of place. Or Shakespeare can start with genuine feelings, as in *Romeo and Juliet*, and show them the sport of errors as in a world of farce. Or he can show Bertram seeing better and Angelo getting caught, and still keep us uncomfortably alert to the precariousness of social existence. Or he can take a Gloucester who in some ways seems to master the wisdom of a dual perspective—a sense of the world as it is, and a loyalty that cannot steer by the world as it is—and show him a more miserable victim than if he were a more rigid man of single-track mind. Or he can take an aged and powerful king, like Lear, and in a secure palace show us that no one is home free, least of all home free from himself. Or he may take a brilliantly and evilly destructive man, like Iago, and by making him charming and plausible and self-defensive—by giving him the amiable demeanor that most men would have, and the apparent justifications that all men need—can subtly bring home to every man that Iago lies within himself. Thus he provides one of the essential experiences of the true community: the knowledge not only that the indispensable common order of life may always be injured or broken, but that all the threats to its wellbeing exist in all of us.

The sense of community, when it is sound, gives men an equal sense of order and of disruptive forces. Surely that is conveyed again and again in the body of Shakespeare's work. We share in that as we share in him, whether in private contemplation or public ceremonial; what is shared belongs neither to professionals nor to masses, neither to ritual solemnities nor to casual delights, neither to past nor present, but embraces all. A body of texts diversely incorporating the vision of a single man often creates a community, and a reverent one; but each community tends to pass, one divinity to yield to another. After four hundred years Shakespeare appears not to be losing but to be extending his dominion. In pondering what it is that he gives that accounts for his gain in power, we have suggested that it is not codes or support or even what we call truth, but the vision of a larger world of actuality and possibility, a completing of ourselves, an awareness of transcendental forces in unexplained and irreducible images; an entry into community that indulges no more than it exacts, that is spacious enough to invite and stir, but never to lull, consciousness. All these experiences, we have kept saying, have a religious quality. The shortcomings in this analogy will be plain to all who wish to question it; yet it may have some suggestive value. Insofar as it is valid, it will serve to imply the range of this body of art, the needs to which it ministers, and the burdens that, without knowing it, we lay on this maker.

Nature and Nothing

BY NORTHROP FRYE

CRITICISM exists because literature is endlessly fascinating, and one of the things that is fascinating about literature is the sense of the oracular that we get from it. The fascination that the fool or the madman had for primitive societies was based on the feeling that when the ordinary consciousness was disordered or put out of action, something mysterious, awful, perhaps divine, could speak in its place. A prophet's "Thus saith the Lord" is much more convincing if he can say little that makes much sense in his own person. Nowadays we have a similar veneration for "creative" minds, the word "creative" being a fossilized religious metaphor, and have developed psychological theories about the creative nature of the subconscious or unconscious parts of the mind. These parts are usually thought of as the lower depths of the mind, corresponding to the oracular caverns of Greek religion. We expect poets to be frequently, if not foolish, at any rate a trifle simple-minded in their ordinary social attitudes, and in their professional function to speak with an involuntary wisdom.

It would be simpler to try to distinguish poetic from discursive thought in a way which does not require the metaphorical intangibles of psychology. The poet's relation to the thinker is similar to his relation to the historian as explained by Aristotle: he establishes the typical or universal constructs of thought, and never, *qua* poet, makes a definite predication. That is, the poet does not define or establish a new and consistent denotation for his words, but deals with the traditional and habitual connotations of words. All directed thinking, when verbal in expression, comes out of a verbal structure already in existence. This structure is not simply a dictionary list of the words we use: it is a network of associative assumptions. Directed thought proceeds by aligning a verbal structure with the events or phenomena that it attempts to describe. Such writing is intentional: it means what it says, because the verbal structure is paralleled with something else. It is the poet's task to articulate the associative structure with which all thinking begins, to use words in their original "ambiguous" sense and not in a particularly defined sense. Poetic thinking is thus not intentional but constructive; it contains meaning, but that meaning is in what the words say as a construct.

In Shakespeare certain words, such as "nature" or "fortune," are repeated with such emphasis that we realize that the meaning of the word is part of the meaning of the play in which it is emphasized. We have also the stock device of a speech turning on the multiple meanings of a word, like Faulconbridge on "commodity" or Ulysses on "degree" and "time." If we did not know English, we should have to look such words up in a dictionary. Since we do know English, we look them up in a kind of imaginary historical dictionary, to see what they would have meant to Shakespeare and his contemporaries. This gives us a meaning which in itself is only commonplace, just as the meaning of such a phrase as "Shut up your doors" or "He has no children" is commonplace when removed from its context. If we try to understand, say, "Shakespeare's conception of nature" as a set of conventional assumptions shared by all his contemporaries, we shall discover, as others have discovered, that Shakespeare was a shallow and obvious philosopher. If we pay more attention to the difference between poetic and other kinds of thought, and deal with such a word only in its specific dramatic contexts, our other and better feeling that Shakespeare's plays take us into the very center of human wisdom will be justified. Here we shall attempt a procedure halfway between the general history of the idea and specific commentary.

Nature, as we ordinarily use the term, means the order of physical existence which forms our environment, the objective or external aspect of our own lives, the world of animals and plants and minerals, surrounded with the sea and the sky. Nature means this in Shakespeare too, of course, but always with its imaginative and poetic overtones. The most important imaginative impact that physical nature has on us is a sense of alienation. There is nothing in it that seems intelligent, moral, or specifically responsive to human needs. Man imposes his own way of life on nature, and transforms it into something with a human shape. There are in consequence two levels of nature: an upper level of human nature and a lower level of physical nature. We are born into the latter world, but do not really belong to it. It is natural to man to be moral, civilized, and socially disciplined; it is unnatural to him to live like the animals. Man's present relation to nature can hardly be expressed except by paradox. Certain human qualities, such as the chastity of Miranda or Marina, are natural, on the human level of nature; the innocence with which animals copulate is natural to them but impossible for human beings. This takes us into the explanation of the two levels of nature given by Christianity, which formed part of a conventional framework of imagery familiar to Shakespeare and to his audience. The nature God had originally planned for man was that of the Golden Age or the Garden of Eden: this was lost at the Fall, but in some measure is recreated by the disciplines of civilization, morality, religion, and the arts. Man is subject to death, and on the physical level of nature there can be no more natural event than death. Yet death was not a part of the order originally planned for man, and in that context death is unnatural, sin even more so.

The circling of the immortal heavenly bodies in the sky is the most eloquent symbol of the order and harmony of the nature that was originally intended for man. The traditional music of the spheres symbolized a harmony that is recreated by human music. Music in Shakespeare has its traditional Platonic meaning of the musical arts, which include poetry (as distinct from the technical arts of painting and architecture), and it also has regularly attached to it the pun on the word "harmony" which makes it a symbol of the original order of nature established for man before the Fall. Shakespeare consistently uses music to represent the order and balance that ought to exist in both individual and social forms of human life. Music is indispensable in restoring sanity to the insane, health to the sick, even life itself to those who, like Thaisa, have temporarily lost it. We recall the famous passage in the fifth act of *The Merchant of Venice* where music is associated with the harmony of the disciplined soul, and the figure of Orpheus, symbolizing the hidden sympathy between man and nature evoked by music and poetry, haunts this and many similar passages in Shakespeare.

As, in Burke's phrase, art is man's nature, the worlds of art and nature are identical on the human level, a fact which helps to account for the vitality of the pastoral convention, the pretence that the simple natural life of the shepherd goes hand in hand with proficiency in music and poetry. The setting of the pastoral is usually designed to suggest the Garden of Eden or the Golden Age. In ordinary life the fact that man essentially belongs to a world with a human shape is symbolized by the garden, the cultivated form of nature. When cultivated, the garden belongs to the human level of nature; when left uncultivated, it relapses to the ordinary physical level. The garden is used as an image of human society with particular emphasis in *Richard II*. The Queen addresses the gardener as "old Adam's likeness," and talks of Eve and the serpent, but this garden is not Eden: it is the ground that Adam had to till after the Fall, and the Queen's attempt to curse it is useless because what is called in *King Lear* the general curse of nature is already there. Hamlet speaks of his time as an unweeded garden possessed by "things rank and gross in nature," but this is the nature of the physical world. When Burgundy in *Henry V* says that the vineyards of France "Defective in their natures, grow to wildness," he is referring to the upper or human level of nature.

The natural state of man, then, is a civilized and ordered state, and the king in particular is the symbol of this order. The better a king he is, the less he is a symbol and the more he is an incarnation of it. "Nature's above art in that respect," says Lear, meaning apparently that kings, like poets, are born and not made. Macbeth's murder of Duncan is a breach in the order of nature, which lets in a destructive force, represented by the tempest-raising witches, and by the prodigies and portents of the murder itself, with which Macbeth allies himself, to his own inevitable destruction. But no king can actually restore mankind to the Golden Age; all around human society is still the lower or physical order of nature. This order moves in circles, imitating the stars in their courses, but its cyclical movement is an amoral force, and it operates by necessity rather than by intelligence and freedom. It produces not only the cycles of seasons and of days, but also, in human life, the cycle of prosperity and decline that is called the wheel of fortune.

In Shakespeare's plays, the histories move almost entirely within the lower cycle or wheel of fortune. The highest point of history is represented by the weeded garden in *Richard II* and by the conquest of "the world's best garden" in *Henry V*. Its lowest point is usually marked by an executed traitor or by a disgraced scapegoat figure like Fastolfe, Falstaff, Pistol, or Exton. Tragedy differs from history in suggesting, more clearly than the histories usually do, some original breaking away from a higher level of nature. In *Antony and Cleopatra*, for example, there is no question of legitimacy or of a sacred anointed king to keep us reminded of the higher kind of order, and the ultimate triumph of Octavius is built into the wheel of fortune, which in a pagan setting is also a wheel of fate. But even there the music of Hercules accompanies the passing of Antony's power, just as the music of Orpheus accompanies the downfall of Queen Catherine in *Henry VIII*. Tragedy also moves down with the descending part of the lower natural cycle, into the darkness of *Macbeth* or the chaos of the storm in *King Lear*. Comedy moves upward with the ascending cycle, but suggests, in a way that history cannot do, a reintegration with the higher level of nature.

In the histories we notice the working of a principle that we might call Proust's law. The only paradises are the paradises we have lost, and every period of history seems to create a pastoral myth out of something in a previous age. The *Henry VI* plays naturally keep looking back to the days of Agincourt; but in the reigns of Henry IV and V too there are plots against the king that look back to the days of Richard as a kind of original social contract, all disasters being blamed on Bolingbroke's violation of this contract. We look back to the days of Richard, and find John of Gaunt taking the same view of the age of Edward III. In *Richard II* itself our sympathies are very evenly divided, because of the conception of nature involved. Richard, as king *de jure*, is the natural head of the state; because he does not do what is required of him in that state, society's natural need for order throws up another natural force in the form of Bolingbroke. Bolingbroke is neither a wicked usurper like Macbeth nor a righteous avenger like Hamlet, but, like Oliver Cromwell in Marvell's poem, a natural force that under certain conditions inevitably makes its appearance. His *de facto* authority, because of society's need of order, becomes *de jure* as well, a fact borne witness to by York's dramatic transfer of loyalties to him.

Still, the transfer of power from Richard to Boling-broke does illustrate a breaking of the connection between human society and the cosmic order, and consequently the deposing of Richard creates a pastoral myth. As soon as Richard becomes impotent, all the magic of music and poetry becomes attached to him, aided by the fact that Richard is a poet himself. Once Henry IV is firmly established as king, he begins to bear the obloquy of responsibility, but neither his effort to dissociate himself from Richard's murder nor his dream of going on a crusade can give his crown the glamour that, in history, only a lost cause can have. Hotspur, with his tremendous energy and egoism, is very well adjusted to nature as an amoral force, the aspect of nature that has been intensified by Henry's accession. His contempt for poetry and music, however, indicates that his instincts are for rebellion and anarchy rather than for order.

His much less likeable conqueror, Prince Henry, succeeds his father legitimately, and so behaves like a *de jure* monarch, even to the extent of describing the plot of Scroop and Grey against him as "Another fall of man," echoing a phrase used by Queen Isabel in the garden scene in *Richard II*. Despite the deep egoism that this phrase suggests, Henry understands the conditions of royalty very well. When his father dies and he is faced with two opposed symbolic father-figures, the Chief Justice and Falstaff, he chooses the right one and rejects the wrong one. His meditations about his father and Richard just before Agincourt betray some uncertainty about his claim to the English throne (to say nothing of the French one, though France hardly counts in the argument), and perhaps some in the audience might have remembered the poignant scene of the death of Mortimer in *1 Henry VI*. Still, it is unnecessary for Henry V to placate his God by building any more chantries for Richard, because he is ascending the wheel of fortune, which does not start turning downward until after his death. Only one phrase, in his speech before Harfleur, "Disguise fair nature with hard-favoured rage," shows any awareness on Henry's part that the level of nature he represents is not the highest possible to man. This glimpse of a better aspect of nature recurs in Burgundy's great speech on the desolation of France already referred to, again in a context which indicates its remoteness. In the world of present action, as Shakespeare presents it in the histories, there is a mixture of two things that are separable when we think of them as past. One is the vision of nature in its original human sense, the cosmic order forfeited by the Fall, an event recalled by every act of treachery or usurpation committed since. The other is nothingness, the abyss of annihilation and nonbeing into which everything, so far as we can see, disappears. Thus the revolving wheel of nature and fortune which is the organizing principle of the histories contains a latent dialectic expressed by the words "nature," in its upper-level sense, and "nothing."

These two words are so prominent in *King Lear* that we may turn to that play to see how tragedy, when emancipated from a historical context and moving in the more autonomous world of myth and folk tale, deals with this dialectic. The abdication scene establishes for us a descent into the lower order of physical nature, a descent symbolized by the act of dividing the kingdom, which in itself would have led to tragedy even if Cordelia had played the role expected of her. Immediately after the abdication we hear Edmund swearing fealty to nature, and we realize that this means nature as an amoral force, the nature symbolized by Edmund's position as Gloucester's "natural" son. Edmund's contempt for astrology is an essential part of his conception of nature as earthbound and as having no attachment to any cosmic order. Edmund, however, has no principle of order within himself, and hence the force he incarnates is, like Macbeth's, purely destructive and self-destructive. The world he helps to bring into being is a world headed towards "nothing." Lear, like Richard, soon discovers that, as man is essentially social, any man's social context is essential to him; hence a king depriving himself of his kingship has given "all," and is left with "nothing." It is impossible for a king to represent only the ideal of kingship, to live with "The name and all th' addition to a king," as Lear proposes to do. Similarly Richard, faced with the logic of Bolingbroke's revolution, which also began by proposing to leave him with the royal title, says:

Make me, that nothing have, with nothing grieved,
And thou with all pleased, that hast all achieved!

But in the lower order of nature there are some remnants of the original order. These are chiefly the society-forming instincts, the emotions of love and loyalty. The traditional symbol of a vestigial state of innocence in ordinary life is the child, for whom love and loyalty are essentials. The representative of this simple and instinctive side of nature in *King Lear* is another "natural," the Fool. The Fool, like the child, has a certain license to see and comment on the simple truth of the situation in front of him, just as Cordelia, Lear's one real child, had done earlier, without the license. The characters in *King Lear* line up on one side or the other of these opposed conceptions of the "natural." The Fool does all he can do, and that is a good deal, to keep Lear anchored on his side, and aware of his community with the "poor naked wretches" who are also abused when order turns to tyranny.

Edgar, of course, is to Edmund what the Fool and Cordelia are to Goneril and Regan. His function in regard to his father is expressed in the phrase "Ripeness is all": he preserves Gloucester through a purgatorial period of attempted suicide until he reaches what is, considering his circumstances, a "natural" death in a state of serenity, even of joy. On the occasions when he speaks in his own person, Edgar assumes a sententious "chorus-character" style not unlike that of a more fully conscious and intelligent Fool. One line in particular, from his last speech (if it is his; the Quartos give it to Albany), indicates the parallel: "Speak what we feel, not what we ought to say." Edgar's relation to Lear is more complex, but extremely important for understanding the conception of nature in the play. Tom o' Bedlam, who eats live frogs and drinks of the frog pond, is in the context of tragedy what Caliban is in comedy and Swift's Yahoo in satire: the naked kernel of the natural man, man shut out from society and therefore from the distinctively human side of his own nature. "Thou art the thing itself," says Lear, contemplating this disconcerting response to his prayer to the poor naked wretches. On the other side of poor Tom are the abysses of nothingness haunted by the foul fiends who possess Tom as they possess Caliban. The vision of Tom o' Bedlam thus represents the bottom of Lear's descent into nature, a perilous path to walk on as he enters the valley of the shadow.

In comedy there is a tension between the natural and the social: in a comedy of manners, where there is a strong element of satire, society is presented as unnatural, as grotesque or ridiculous or hypocritical. The audience itself is assumed to be a natural society, possessed of an integrity and common sense that most of the characters in the play lack. A purely ironic comedy, like most of Chekhov's, preserves this tension of audience and theatrical society to the end. Shakespeare never attempted this kind of comedy (*Troilus and Cressida* does something quite different), which with its pervading sense of society as a spectacle, held up to be gazed at, seems to belong more naturally to the proscenium theatre. Shakespeare remains faithful to the normal conclusion of comedy, where the characters who most closely represent the audience's attitude, usually the hero and the heroine, triumph over the unnatural society of the play, and bring as much as possible of that society into reconciliation with them. In *The Taming of the Shrew* Katharina's obedience is more natural than her shrewishness, not because of any moral difference between them, but because, as obedient wife, she is less obviously easy to regard as ridiculous, and is less of an obstacle to the festive conclusion. What then becomes of her shrewishness? Theoretically at least, it has disappeared: she is changed, her father says, as she had never been. Thus the action of comedy begins in a world of illusion and moves toward a separation of the natural, or at least the more natural, from the nonexistent. The more romantic the comedy, the more closely the natural society reached at the end approximates the upper level of nature.

This last point indicates a complicating factor in comedy. The lower order of nature, the physical world we live in and the human society adapted to it, is simply there, the reality-principle. But no matter how fully we may realize our own human natures by social discipline, there will always be a still higher order of nature which is not there, but which is desirable. As comedy normally moves toward the desirable, its action includes a good deal of what is not merely unlikely but, in terms of the nature we live in, unnatural. In the daylight world of the histories,

Owen Glendower's interest in magic looks merely like a neurotic obsession. But comedy, which deals with what we want, has much to do with the world of dreams and hopes and wishes, and hence in the comedies magic may have a functional role, as have fairies, identical twins, substituted brides, and lost-and-found princesses. In real life it is seldom that things turn out "right," yet our use of the word "right" indicates that the unlikely, when desirable, has its nature too.

Comedy, then, usually begins with a social situation which, however "really there" it may be, is presented as undesirable, absurd or ridiculous, and hence as having something in it which is unnatural. A harsh father forbids his daughter to marry the obviously right man, or someone with authority plunges himself into some obsession, like Leontes, with potentially disastrous results. The action moves toward a "happy ending" or festive conclusion which is more desirable and more in accordance with what the audience sees to be common sense. There is an interchange of reality and illusion: what is presented as real at the outset disappears; what was at the beginning only a hope or wish realizes itself. The conception of nature that we have dealt with thus far helps us to see this action as a movement from a lower to a higher level of nature, or from an artificial society (in the modern sense of artificial) to a natural society. This natural society, of course, is far removed from the eighteenth-century conceptions of that phrase that we may be more familiar with. And perhaps we can revise a sentence two paragraphs back to read: the more romantic the comedy, the more closely the natural society reached at the end approximates the regained Golden Age or lost paradise of man.

We saw from the example of the Fool in *King Lear* that there is a kind of "natural" behavior which is somewhat like the kind idealized in the eighteenth century: primitive, simple, unspoiled, and instinctively loyal and affectionate. The Fool suggests two other character types, the child and the professional clown. Children are not much featured in Shakespeare, except as amateur clowns like Moth in *Love's Labour's Lost* and Robin in *The Merry Wives of Windsor*. The child is associated with innocence, and innocence in an adult would be a form of "natural" behavior which is instinctively obedient to the higher nature of man, however much at odds with the lower nature around it. A very clear example is the chastity of Marina in the brothels of Mytilene. Female chastity is in fact Shakespeare's usual image of innocence, just as the traditional child's innocence has much to do with sexual inexperience. The affinity between chastity and the harmony of unfallen nature, so much dwelt on in Milton's *Comus*, is already present in the Shakespeare romances.

Most of the lesser fairies in *The Midsummer Night's Dream* have a childlike quality about them, as do, more obviously, the disguised fairies in *The Merry Wives*. The Robin of this play, just referred to, is called "Jack-a-Lent" and has the same name as the boy-fairy Puck. Fairies are also devoted to chastity, as Falstaff discovers to his cost. Fairies are elemental spirits, and elemental spirits are in the physical world what children, regarded as symbols of innocence, are in the ordinary human world: remnants of an original "true consent," as Milton calls it, with the cosmic order. The control of elemental spirits, or magic, is thus an essential part of the music and poetry that are attributes of the higher nature of man.

In most of Shakespeare's comedies the action is presented as a collision of two societies. One is an obstructive or anti-comic society, often equipped with some kind of harsh law that threatens the happiness or even the life of the main characters. Shylock, Duke Frederick, Theseus, Solinus, Angelo, all invoke or administer the laws of such societies. Sometimes it is represented simply by an unsympathetic father or by some quirk of perverseness or melancholy in one of the central characters (Proteus, Bertram, Ferdinand of Navarre, and, of course, Katharina). As the action of comedy moves toward the fulfillment of love, this anti-comic society is nearly always concerned to roughen the course of true love. The other society, which brings about the festive conclusion, is a natural society in the paradoxical sense that we have been studying. That is, it is associated with music, magic, chastity, fairies, dreams, and improbable but fortunate events.

In some of the comedies this natural society is located in a forest or similar pastoral setting: the three forest comedies, *The Two Gentlemen of Verona*, *As You Like It*, and *A Midsummer Night's Dream*, show the shape of the action very clearly. We begin with a society based on some kind of obstacle to the happiness of the young lovers, and thence move into a forest where the comic resolution is achieved. In *A Midsummer Night's Dream*, and in *As You Like It* to a lesser extent, the forest is a world of magic, and in *The Two Gentlemen of Verona* it is a world of Robin-Hood-like adventurers who give more the impression of being released from social inhibitions than of being actual criminals. We notice that in all three plays the society of the forest world is at least equal in rank to that of the anti-comic one. The robbers in *The Two Gentlemen* are all exiled noblemen; at the center of the forest of Arden is the senior Duke; the fairies have their own king and queen. The effect of this equality is to carry through the comic resolution without disturbing the social ranks of the original anti-comic society. In *Love's Labour's Lost* the roles of the two societies are reversed: the pastoral retreat of the four nobles is the anti-comic society. This is connected with the fact that this play does not reach the normal comic resolution.

In the three forest comedies the forest society begins in a state of antagonism to the anti-comic one, being outlawed, exiled, or beyond the reach of the "sharp Athenian law." At the end of the play it has taken over its rival and informed it with its own comic spirit, just as outlawed impulses in the mind do in a wish-fulfillment dream. In other plays it is simply the union of two separated and equal societies, one of them exiled or outcast at the beginning, that brings about the comic ending. Ephesus in *A Comedy of Errors* has passed a law killing all Syracusans, but of course it is the arrival of the complementary Syracusan twins that saves Aegeon and winds up the play. In *Twelfth Night* the two separated societies are those of Orsino and Olivia, united by the twins from the sea, where the *Comedy of Errors* theme of perilous landing reappears briefly in the story of Antonio.

In other comedies the pro-comic or natural society is associated with some kind of curative or healing power which is applied to the anti-comic one. Petruchio, whose rough magic charms Katharina into adjusting to marriage, has something of a "doctor" role—not the *dottore* of the *commedia dell'arte* but the doctor of those plays of Molière in which the right man is the only cure needed for an allegedly sick heroine. The fairy-forest appears briefly at the conclusion of *The Merry Wives* in a curative role, expelling the lust of Falstaff and the avarice of Page. In a much more serious comedy, *All's Well That Ends Well*, Helena's power of curing the King of France makes her the focus of the natural society. Since Helena is inferior in social rank to Bertram, this play seems an exception to the rule that the two societies are always equal in rank, but the exception is only in Bertram's mind, as the King of France makes clear.

In *The Merchant of Venice* the natural society of

Portia's house in Belmont faces the Venice of Shylock with its very different conception of the value of gold. In this house, as in the forest of Oberon, magic, music, and the harmony of the spheres form part of the triumph of love and friendship. In *Measure for Measure* the anti-comic society is centered on Angelo, and the disguised Duke is the complementary focus. Around him gather the victims of Angelo's anti-comic legalism, and with these victims the Duke returns at the end in the regular reversal of fortune. In this play, as in *All's Well*, the two societies are in the same place, not in two different ones, so that the contrast between them is expressed by the spirit and attitude of what is said rather than by the conventional imagery of magic or forest or fairy.

All through the comedies we can see the spirit of the natural or pro-comic society catching, like fire in kindling, on certain spots. One of these spots is the clown or fool, whose licensed speech is essential to the spirit of comedy. Another is the song, often associated with the clown, which with its music helps to focus and intensify the comic mood. In Shakespearean comedy, where the unmusical is so closely associated with the villainous or the absurd, it is hardly possible to imagine what an anti-comic song would be like: in any case there are none. The great *aubade* in *Cymbeline* is sung to Imogen at the behest of Cloten after she has unconsciously spent a night with Iachimo, but Cloten's indifference to its beauty and the fact that it is doing his suit no good are both obvious. A song may be sung in an ironic or melancholy context, like the spring and winter songs at the end of *Love's Labour's Lost*, with its postponed happy ending, or "Who is Sylvia?" sung by the fickle Proteus to the wrong girl while the right one is listening, but the emotional effect of the song is always to throw us forward to the comic conclusion.

The progress of the comic action is not a simple one, but follows the dialectical pattern already mentioned. As the action moves from a lower to a higher level of the natural, the latter pulls away from a world which, left to itself, becomes amorphous. We may call this, the world of "nothing" left behind, a sense of lost identity. As the comic resolution is taking shape, we pass through a phase marked by impenetrable disguises, confusions, misunderstandings, and menaces. There is a pervading theme, even in quite lighthearted comedies, of madness or death, or both. The theme of death hangs over not only the somber *Measure for Measure*, but *The Merchant of Venice* and *A Comedy of Errors* as well, and the accusation of madness is prominently featured in *Twelfth Night* and *A Midsummer Night's Dream*.

In the four romances with which Shakespeare's work concludes, the separation of higher nature from nothing is at its clearest. In *Pericles* the two worlds, as noted by Wilson Knight, are symbolized by music and tempest. A world presided over by the providence of Diana, and associated with music, the chastity of Marina, and the magical healing powers of

Cerimon, separates from the unreality of shipwreck and incest and treachery and venereal disease. In *Cymbeline* the growing point of the natural society is the cave of Belarius, again associated with magic, music, and the preservative potion given Imogen by Pisanio, in place of the death demanded by both the Queen and Posthumus. When the society of this cave emerges, the opposed society dominated by the Queen and Cloten dissolves. In *The Winter's Tale* the focus of the natural society is the pastoral world of Bohemia, with another focus in Paulina's house, where Hermione's life has been preserved. The union of Perdita and Hermione, like the union of Marina and Thaisa in *Pericles*, separates the comic society from the mirage of Leontes' jealousy. Leontes, Camillo says prophetically:

> o'er and o'er divides him
> 'Twixt his unkindness and his kindness; th' one
> He chides to hell and bids the other grow
> Faster than thought or time.

The last phrase indicates that the world of higher nature which romance approaches is also a world not of time but of the fulfillment of time, the kind of fulfillment traditionally symbolized by the perpetual spring of paradise.

In *The Tempest* the world of shipwreck and treachery has largely spent its force before the action of the play begins, Prospero and Miranda having been preserved in being by Gonzalo many years before. The

entire action thus takes place within the natural society, which is controlled by Prospero's magic, and has
the usual associations of music and chastity. Here
Caliban represents what Tom 'o Bedlam represented
in tragedy, the fiend-haunted natural man whom
Prospero is trying to raise to a better level of nature.
The dialectical action comes to its climax in the
masque of elemental spirits presented to Ferdinand
and Miranda. The theme of the masque is the marriage of the lovers, and the imagery is that of a para-
disal perpetual spring. No other scene in Shakespeare
displays such a concentration of images of a "golden
world," to use a phrase from *As You Like It*. But then
Prospero speaks, the spell is broken, and the scene van-
ishes. There follows Prospero's great speech over the
vanishing of everything in time, which seems both a
curious anticlimax to the wedding masque and somewhat overresonant as a sequel to its delicate fantasy.
In the context of our present argument we can see it
as the point in Shakespearean comedy where the separation of nature and nothing is at its clearest.

But there is another aspect to the scene which
brings the speech following the masque into focus.
The masque is a work of music and drama, summoned
up by Prospero to enact his present fancies. The
speech, like the very different time-speech of Ulysses
in *Troilus and Cressida*, presents us with the total annihilation of everything in time which is the first fact
of ordinary life. Thus the dialectic of nature and nothing in Shakespeare turns out to be also the dialectic of

art and life, art being identical with nature on its higher level, and guaranteeing, more clearly than any myth of a lost paradise, a reality in our lives that is clear of the dissolving chaos of experience. In this scene the interchange of reality and illusion has completed itself. We go out of the theatre into "real life" again, which we know now to be also an illusion because of a reality that we have glimpsed for an instant in the illusion of the play.

Shakespeare's Nomenclature

BY HARRY LEVIN

W HEN Juliet asks, "What's in a name?" she assumes that the question is rhetorical. Her implicit answer, if it were voiced, would be, "Little or nothing." But her concrete example is ambiguous:

> That which we call a rose
> By any other name would smell as sweet.

It may be a case in point that the sweetest of all names, for Romeo up to a few moments before, has been Rosaline. Now he is quite willing to forget it in favor of the sweeter Juliet. Shakespeare had made earlier amends for this neglect when he gave the name of Rosaline to the sprightly heroine of *Love's Labour's Lost;* and, in the slightly modified form of Rosalind, he glorified it with the irresistible heroine of *As You Like It.* Even she, however, has her detractors. "I do not like her name," says the melancholy Jaques. To which the lover Orlando wryly retorts, "There was no thought of pleasing you when she was christened." Names, then, are matters of personal taste to which reactions can vary. Romeo sounds propitious to Juliet's nurse because it alliterates with rosemary—rosemary for remembrance, if not for Rosaline—even though it is also the dog's letter, a snarling omen, *rrr!* To Mercutio the lovelorn Romeo seems as lank as a herring without its roe; what is left of him can be no more than a lover's sigh: *-meo, -meo, O me!* (That wordplay, such as it is, would have been spoiled if Shakespeare had not Italianized the Latin ending of the original Romeus in Arthur Brooke's poem, through which he had acquainted himself with the tale.) To "be some other name" is to be a stranger. So, in *King John*, the newly knighted Bastard resolves to snub his former cronies:

And if his name be George, I'll call him Peter.

Would Romeo retain his dear perfection without his existing name, as Juliet affirms? "I doubt it," Wilson Knight has succinctly commented. "Try Iachimo." Professor Knight's suggestion is worth the experiment:

O Iachimo, Iachimo! wherefore art thou Iachimo?

We need not presume that there is something innate in certain vocables which makes the villain of *Cymbeline* a fitting companion for Iago; but Romeo has a sound, for Professor Knight, which is simultaneously Roman, romantic, and suggestive of roaming. Within a few moments Juliet comes to adore the repetition of the name, and within a day Romeo comes to believe that it can have a murderous impact. Yet the really dangerous appellation, after all, is not his forename but his surname. "What's Montague?" One of the noblest families in Verona, to its members and to some of their fellow citizens. To others, especially to the Capulets, it is a rallying cry for tribal antagonisms. Shakespeare balances the rival claims with symmetry and objectivity by making them metrically equivalent: *Montague/ Capulet, Romeo Montague/ Juliet Capulet*. Similarly, he plays no favorites as between the two complaisant school friends of Hamlet. Each has his interchangeable amphimacer.

Thanks, Rosencrantz and gentle Guildenstern,

says the King, to which the Queen adds:

Thanks, Guildenstern and gentle Rosencrantz.

Juliet—on that night in the orchard, at any rate, before the lovers are overtaken by the swift fatalities they have challenged—is a nominalist. That is to say, she believes in the immediacy of experience and the uniqueness of individuals rather than in classes, categories, or generalizations.

So is Falstaff: he is the very nominalist of nominalists when he reduces honor to a word, and that word to a breath of air. Since that word is a fighting word for Hotspur, it is a transcendent reality by which men live and die. Insofar as words can be realities, Juliet was wrong; there can be all too much in a name, as she will find out all too soon. Good name means considerably more than an illusory image to Cassio, to Desdemona, and finally to Othello; it is a jewel of the soul, the loss of which spells tragedy. What becomes there involved is social repute, not simple denomination. Yet how much of the atmosphere in Shakespeare's plays is already conveyed to us when we scan his *dramatis personae!* True, he is not so erudite a philologist as most of his commentators. John Ruskin, who had more Greek, paused in the midst of his unfinished treatise on political economy, *Munera Pulveris*, to hold an etymological inquest over Ophelia and other Greek-rooted names. Thereupon Matthew Arnold took exception to Ruskin's digression for its "note of provinciality," its lack of moderation and proportion. It is not clear at this distance, a century afterward, just who was being provincial. Ruskin felt that he had made a discovery, to which he kept returning in side remarks, but Arnold's counterthrust was sharp enough to deter him from the special investigation he promised.

Arnold, surprisingly for a major English critic, has no light to throw upon Shakespeare, and not much sweetness. Others abode Arnold's question; Shakespeare, in Arnold's obscurantist phrase, overtopped knowledge; and their conjunction leaves us where the Romantics stood, gazing in uncritical awe at the inscrutable handiwork of a natural genius. During the last hundred years we have been learning to examine Shakespeare more and more closely. On the whole he has withstood that scrutiny, and rewarded it with a renewed awareness of his insight and technique. Today we think of him as a highly conscious artist. Being only human and writing for set occasions, he had his lapses and he made his compromises; but he nods far less frequently than his critics, whose principal activity has been to catch one another napping; and we are likely to understand him better if we assume that he knew what he was doing every minute, even at the risk of an occasional exercise in overingenuity on our part. Professor Knight may be considering too curiously when he suggests that Alonso connotes aloneness, or that the Prince of Aragon is designated *ex officio* as arrogant, or that the pirates Menas and Menecrates are threatening figures because they have minatory names. But his intensive kind of curiosity has done much to underline the patterns and highlight the details of Shakespeare's artistry, and we should feel indebted to him for reviving Juliet's question in his volume of essays, *The Sovereign Flame*.

It should have been a secure assumption that names, like most of the other components in language and life, meant a great deal to Shakespeare. Yet criticism was set back by Arnold's caveat. Except for one or two German dissertations, which are hardly more than annotated listings, plus a few articles on specific lines of derivation, the field of Shakespearean nomenclature is wide open, and constitutes an inviting pasture to browse in. Meanwhile there has been wider realization that the naming of characters is a serious—albeit subordinate—feature of literary art, and that it is susceptible to analysis by linguistic science—more specifically, by that branch of it which bears the name of onomatology, and which, if it does not intimidate us, can illuminate our concern. Nothing is ever completely random in the artistic process. Providence, as Ruskin put it, is tempered by "cunning purpose." Much may be unconscious, to be sure; and some of it, being inherent in the material, may not express the artist himself. But, to state it categorically, the *persona* begins with the name; it is as much part of character as the mask in ancient drama; and when it is not handed down from a myth or some other source, it may be taken as the expression of a writer's own intention. Hence a realistic novelist, like Flaubert, would take the same sort of care with names that he did with dress or milieu. They had to be real names, characteristic only in that they sounded right for the people who bore them.

At the other and older extreme, which goes back at least as far as to Homer, we have the name that stands by itself as a characterization. Though we have no vernacular phrase for this device of language, such as the German *sprechende Namen,* "speaking names," a technical term has been coined, so that we may talk of charactonyms. Such are the abstract labels of the moralities, which Shakespeare was not above recalling, like the Vice Iniquity and Lady Vanity. Such usages were reinforced by the Puritan habit of deriving Christian names from moral qualities. Temperance, sneers Antonio in *The Tempest*, "Temperance was a delicate wench." It takes a Bunyan to confer flesh and blood upon a Mr. Greatheart or a Mr. Badman, but the "Mr." always helps to humanize the situation. In the long comic tradition where the charactonym flourished, it gradually evolved from the sphere of morals to that of manners, and by way of Ben Jonson to the Restoration and the eighteenth century. Knights are in particular evidence here, since they have the privilege of sporting double-barrelled names: Sir Politick Wouldbe, Sir Fopling Flutter, Sir Benjamin Backbite. But the ladies hold their own: Lady Sneerwell, Lady Wishfort (in words of one syllable, "Wish for't"). And Mrs. Malaprop's name, so neatly adapted from *mal à propos*, is no less inspired than her classic abuse of the King's English.

The resourceful namer tends to use metonymy rather than personification: in other words, to single out the vivid attribute rather than to fall back on the pallid abstraction. Thus Tom Jones's tutor is named Thwackum, since he so roundly exerts his tutorial prerogative. Tom's own name embodies straightforward typicality, as deliberately contrasted with Sir Charles Grandison, where the pretentious note is sounded by the first syllable of the surname. With the increase of realism and the decline of allegory, there is a tendency to leave the meaning somewhat latent, so that it seems to be rather a marginal comment than a heraldic flourish. Heathcliff, for instance, has the air of a perfectly plausible cognomen; yet what more compelling designation could we hit upon for the forces unleashed in *Wuthering Heights?* The author of *Vanity Fair*, not surprisingly in view of his title, hints at the personalities of his puppets: Becky Sharp, Lord Steyne (stain). He even indulges in a caricaturist's dalliance with such eighteenth-century appellatives as Bareacres, for a penniless lord, and Yellowplush, for a strutting lackey. Yet Thackeray held, among his many reservations on Dickens, that "Micawber appears to me the exaggeration of a name, as the name is of a man."

Now many of Dickens' names are self-characterizing: Pecksniff, Veneering, Bounderby. We could not, by any stretch of the nomenclatorial license, call Scrooge Cheeryble or the Cheeryble brothers the Scrooges. Others, like Micawber itself or Pickwick, are merely odd; yet they serve, in spite of Thackeray's cavil, to bring out individual eccentricities; and some of those inventions have become eponyms, in the sense that the name has become a byword for a peculiar pattern of behavior. Commonly we speak of persons or actions as Pickwickian or Micawberish. Shakespeare made such a joke over Benedick in *Much Ado about Nothing* that that recalcitrant bachelor ended by becoming the eponymous patron of all married men. Comparably, Romeo became the generic lover, Shylock the extortionist, Falstaff the trencherman, Puck the jokester, and so on. Dickens borrowed his Pickwick from a sign on a passing van; other names he jotted down from placards and tombstones, keeping those lists which have been reprinted in Forster's biography. Henry James moreover worked with lists culled from his daily reading of the London *Times*, seeking in them—as in everything else—a certain style, an Anglo-American tone; but there are some occasions on which he was more explicit, as with Mr. Newman on the one hand or Prince Amerigo on the other.

The perfect name could be defined as combining a literal authenticity with a symbolic purport. However, the gamut ranges widely between those extremes, and Shakespeare ranges up and down the gamut. Certainly he inherited as much as he invented, and here the interest lies in his handling of the conventional associations. Melville employed Scriptural names—Ishmael, Ahab—to convey the effect of prefiguration, the feeling that all this has happened before and will inevitably happen again. Joyce, by christening his spokesman Stephen Dedalus, provided him with both a tutelary saint and a classical prototype. So the virgin goddess Diana, whose cult is celebrated in *Pericles*, has an Elizabethan godchild in the maiden Diana of *All's Well That Ends Well*; and the Roman Portia—Cato's daughter, Brutus' wife in *Julius Caesar* —has a civic-minded namesake in *The Merchant of Venice*, whom Ruskin, with the casket scenes in mind, would connect with "portion." Later characterizations, in like fashion, have been prefigured by Shakespeare's. Hamlet's jester Yorick is the legendary an-

cestor of Parson Yorick in Tristram Shandy, while
in turn Trollope's Mr. Slope claims descent from
Sterne's Dr. Slop. "Of Yorick," remarks Professor
Knight, "all I can say is that it fits." That impression
of fitness, which begs the question somewhat, is a tes-
timonial to Shakespeare's aptness for making names
fit, for using them as keys to memorable characters.

They must be chosen out of the available vocabulary in order to be fitted into the dramatic context.
Yet, since form follows function here as elsewhere,
perhaps I should discuss some of their uses before dis-
cussing some of Shakespeare's choices. It should almost go without saying that his word-conscious
world is a name-conscious world, where conflict is
fought out by name-calling and status is conferred by
name-dropping. In that respect, its logical culmination
is the account of Princess Elizabeth's baptism at the
end of *Henry VIII.* This name-consciousness mani-
fests itself in the usual habits of paranomasia. To
judge from Falstaff's recollection, John of Gaunt has
been destined to go through life hearing puns on his
name; and he himself, by punning on his deathbed, invites the sarcasm of Richard II:

Can sick men play so nicely with their names?

In *The Merry Wives of Windsor* the camouflaged
Master Ford appropriately masks himself as Master
Brook; and Falstaff, whose immersion in a ford will be
a further chance to quibble, responds to a draught of
sack from his visitor: "Such brooks are welcome to

me, that o'erflows such liquor." Inasmuch as punning is a triumph of sheer material circumstance over the reason, it may be a grim reduction to existential absurdity, as in the Second Part of *Henry VI,* where York pronounces:

> For Suffolk's Duke, may he be suffocate.

The prophecy that the Duke of Suffolk will meet his death by water turns out to be an equivocation on the forename of his assassin, Walter Whitmore. The foreordained malefactor in *Richard III,* whose name starts with a G, turns out to be not George, Duke of Clarence, but Richard, Duke of Gloucester. Oracles, like charades, take delight in such unexpected confrontations and unlikely materializations.

Satire, when it presents real characters and events, usually changes their names in the interests of discretion. When Hamlet presents a dramatization of his father's murder, he calls the victim Gonzago and implies that any resemblance to actual persons, living or dead, is purely coincidental. In comedy, which thrives upon confusions, to mistake a person is to get his name wrong. The pairs of identical twins in *The Comedy of Errors* could not be confounded for very long, if there were not two Dromios and two Antipholuses. But mistaken identity can be tragic as well as comic. There is no grimmer scene in *Julius Caesar* than the one in which a certain Cinna—an innocent man, in fact a poet—is confused with Cinna the conspirator and found guilty by nominal association. "I am Cinna the poet," he plaintively cries, but it makes no difference to the angry plebeians. "Tear him for his bad verses," then they shout, and hustle him away to his death. What's in a name indeed! It can operate as a disguise, when a character is engaged in eluding identification, such as Cesario, Bellario, or Sebastian. It can thereby show a sense of decorum, as with Florizel, the flowery prince of *The Winter's Tale*, who is addressed as Doricles in the pastoral episodes. Again it can show a sense of humor, as with Feste, the festive clown of *Twelfth Night*, whose mock-priest is addressed as Sir Topas, presumably after the mock-knight of Chaucer.

When Celia flees to the forest in *As You Like It*, she announces that her *nom de guerre* will be

Something that hath a reference to my state.

Accordingly she becomes Aliena, the alien one, the fair stranger. Rosalind, her fellow traveller, still rather girlish though disguised as a boy, is accordingly known as Ganymede after Jupiter's epicene favorite. In *Cymbeline*, when Imogen is forced to disguise herself, she emerges as the semi-allegorical Fidele. "Thy name well fits thy faith," she is told, "thy faith thy name." The moral pose can be carried too far, as everything is in *Titus Andronicus*, where Tamora and her two sons introduce themselves to the demented Titus as Revenge and Rape and Murder respectively *in propria persona*, a troop of pale shades from the older moralities. Of much greater significance is the agnomen, the honorific name of Caius Marcius, who is hailed as Coriolanus by virtue of his bravery at Corioli; for it is at Corioli that, with a hollow reverberation, Coriolanus is fated to die. Through the other two Roman plays we watch the private name of Caesar becoming a synonym for emperor, and the root for *kaiser* or *tsar*. It is more than a verbal transference when a country is personified by its monarch, when Cleopatra herself is saluted as Egypt. Whereas to speak of the Dane is to underscore one of the innumerable questions raised by *Hamlet:* who is the Dane? is it the King or the Prince or the Ghost?

Worldly preferment is often signalized, in Shakespearean parlance, by "addition," as when the hierarchic ascent of Macbeth is heralded by the tantalizing salute of the Witches: Thane of Glamis, Thane of Cawdor, King of Scotland. In the course of that ascent Macbeth itself becomes

A hotter name than any is in hell.

The transitoriness of such ambitions comes out strongly in the First Part of *Henry VI* with the prolonged and sonorous inquiry:

Where is the great Alcides of the field,
Valiant Lord Talbot, Earl of Shrewsbury,
Created for his rare success in arms
Great Earl of Washford, Waterford, and Valence,
Lord Talbot of Goodrig and Urchinfield,

Lord Strange of Blackmere, Lord Verdun of Alton,
Lord Cromwell of Wingfield, Lord Furnival of Shef-
    field,
The thrice-victorious Lord Falconbridge,
Knight of the noble order of Saint George,
Worthy Saint Michael, and the Golden Fleece;
Great Marshal to Henry the Sixth
Of all his wars within the realm of France?

Where indeed? Where is he now? *Ubi est?* Joan of
Arc—or Joan la Pucelle, as Shakespeare styles her,
with innuendos on Pucelle or virgin—levels the feudal
hierarchies with her vulgar retort:

> Here is a silly-stately style indeed!
> The Turk, that two-and-fifty kingdoms hath,
> Writes not so tedious a style as this.
> Him that thou magnifi'st with all these titles
> Stinking and flyblown lies here at our feet.

Falstaff is well nigh out-Falstaffed in Joan's reduction
of honor to a breath. The magniloquence of the
Turk, the exotic coloring of the Levant, the distant
place-names of Asia and Africa had contributed to the
geographic impetus of Marlowe's tragedies. Shakespeare could ridicule those effects in the fustian of Ancient Pistol: "Have we not Hiren here?" He could
likewise cultivate them at need, as in *Antony and
Cleopatra* when the potentates of the East are mus-
tered out in full panoply:

> Bocchus, the King of Libya; Archelaus,
> Of Cappadocia; Philadelphos, king
> Of Paphlagonia; the Thracian king, Adallas;
> King Malchus of Arabia; King of Pont;
> Herod of Jewry; Mithridates, king
> Of Commagene; Polemon and Amyntas,
> The kings of Mede and Lycaonia, with a
> More larger list of sceptres.

Roll-calls and casualty lists, like the catalogues of epic, set the scene and dramatize the issues, whether in Mediterranean antiquity or in the British past.

> I had an Edward, till a Richard kill'd him;
> I had a Harry, till a Richard kill'd him:
> Thou hadst an Edward, till a Richard kill'd him;
> Thou hadst a Richard, till a Richard kill'd him,

laments the dowager Queen Margaret to the dowager Queen Elizabeth in *Richard III;* and the litany, with its familiar and repeated names, suggests that—though dynasties pass—there will always be an England. The implication becomes an affirmation, suggesting as it does firm dynastic stability, when the new King Henry reassures his brothers:

> This is the English, not the Turkish court;
> Not Amurath an Amurath succeeds,
> But Harry Harry.

There the shift from Islamic to Christian names brings matters home directly to Shakespeare's audience, as he so frequently liked to do.

Whether he drew upon foreign or domestic history, history converging on mythology or legend at all events, he had to play the game with traditional counters. Tragedy, to a larger degree, and comedy, almost wholly, offered him the freedom to characterize and to coin. We turn, then, from the functional aspect of names to the problem of selection, a terrain no less broad and vague than Shakespeare's European geography, with its Bohemian seacoast and Danish cliffs. Its general flavor is more or less Italianate, as the Elizabethans conceived of Italy, glamorous and sinister by turns. Verona furnishes the setting for both a comedy and a tragedy. Its prince is Escalus, which is a Latinized variant of the ruling family's name, della Scala. Its two gentlemen are Valentine, whose connotations are those of the perennially faithful lover, and Proteus, who is assuredly protean in the moods and changes of his heart. Neither sounds especially Veronese—any more than that model of Old French courtliness, Sir Eglamour. Some of Shakespeare's Italian names are the standard ones accorded to minor parts in grand opera (Claudio for the juvenile lead in both *Much Ado about Nothing* and *Measure for Measure*). Others have undeniably English overtones. Mercutio is nothing if not mercurial; and Romeo's confidant, Benvolio, is his tried and true well-wisher. The exact opposite of the latter is Malvolio, an envious detractor with a jaundiced outlook, nominally resembling Malevole, the satiric reformer in Marston's *Malcontent*.

The riddle of Maria's forged love letter—M.O.A.I.

—seems to be based upon certain key letters in Malvolio's name. It also comes alphabetically close to the names of the two heroines in *Twelfth Night:* if you play anagrams, add one letter to Viola, scramble, and you get Olivia; add another letter, allow one substitution, and you get Malvolio. Sir Toby Belch, the apostle of cakes and ale, whose name is too often interpreted as a stage direction, and Sir Andrew Aguecheek, the knight of the quaking countenance—not to mention the vicar of *As You Like It*, Sir Oliver Martext—take their stand in the staunch old English humorous tradition. Ben Jonson strengthened that tradition decisively when he Anglicized *Every Man in His Humour*, shifting the locale from Florence to London and renaming his Italian characters. Shakespeare juxtaposes the two backgrounds in *The Taming of the Shrew*, where Christopher (or Christophero) Sly, the tinker of the Induction, is more in his element with Marian Hacket, the fat ale-wife of Wincot, than in watching the play-within-the-play. This performance is all the more theatrical because it is supposed to occur in Padua, yet Petruchio's servants seem to be Sly's compatriots: Curtis and Ralph and Sugarsop and the rest. One of them, Grumio, seems to be an Anglo-Italian groom.

The comic servant in *The Merchant of Venice*, too, has an Italian name with an English undertone. Launcelot is a romantic improvement on its naïve predecessor, Launce in *The Two Gentlemen of Verona*. Gobbo might be Venetian; but it also approximates "gobble," along with Shylock's epithet for his servingman, "a huge feeder." Shakepeare found an Old Testament name for Tubal, the Venetian Jew, as well as for Aaron, the Moor of *Titus Andronicus*. As for Shylock, he has been traced to Shalach, one of the minor progeny of Shem. The Hebrew meaning, cormorant, is apt if obscure; but Shakespeare makes the sound convey a meaning of its own, compounded of sharpness and harshness, so that the name evokes the character by a kind of psychological onomatopoeia. Shakespeare smattered a number of languages, quoted Latin freely, and knew French well enough to perpetrate some outrageous *double-entendres*. Jack Cade can ribaldly allude to Monsieur Basimecu, and Pistol blasphemously take in vain the name of Signor Dew. The cast of *All's Well That Ends Well* includes the clown Lavache—cow being a contemptuous metaphor—and the boastful man of words, Parolles (*paroles*). Among the aristocratic French names in *Love's Labour's Lost*, Moth (pronounced "mote") would pass for an Anglicization of La Motte, while likening its bearer, the diminutive page, to both a delicate insect and a particle of dust. The Constable, Goodman Dull, needs no translation.

The Forest of Arden, where *As You Like It* takes place, is evidently the border region between Belgium and France, the Ardennes; but at the same time it takes us back to the heart of England, Shakespeare's Warwickshire; for Arden was his mother's family name. The denizens of this forest are bucolic shepherds: Corin, Silvius, Phoebe. The hero and his brother are named after two of Charlemagne's doughtiest paladins: an Orlando (*gallice* Roland) for an Oliver. The eccentric Jaques, invoked monosyllabically, echoes a somewhat malodorous pun vented by Sir John Harington in his notorious pamphlet on the introduction of the water-closet, *The Metamorphosis of Ajax*, where the mythic allusion plays on the word for privy, a jakes. There may be a fainter echo in the Ajax of *Troilus and Cressida*. Hence drama involves catharsis in its most literal sense, when Jaques proposes to administer an ethical purge:

> Give me leave
> To speak my mind, and I will through and through
> Cleanse the foul body of th' infected world,
> If they will patiently receive my medicine.

If names can localize and lend concreteness, they can equally well etherealize, as they do by abetting the fantasy of *A Midsummer Night's Dream*. There the principal characters are Greek; the presiding couple are mythological figures, Theseus and Hippolyta. The fairy pair, Titania and Oberon, may well be uneasy in their mixed marriage; for one of them was an Ovidian enchantress, the other an elf-king of medieval romance. Their factotum, Puck or Robin Goodfellow, could scarcely be more English; nor could the names of their most exquisite followers, Mustardseed, Peaseblossom, Cobweb, and Moth. Even less probable is the relationship that precipitates Nick Bottom, the

Weaver, into the arms of the Fairy Queen. His name, with its standing invitation to punsters, actually denotes a tool of his trade, a weaver's skein. The other rude mechanicals—Peter Quince, Francis Flute, Tom Snout, Robin Starveling, and Snug the Joiner—assist in the transposition from Athens to London.

If we compare *King Lear* with the old play that Shakespeare adapted, we can see that he made a fairly consistent attempt to historicize his fairy-tale subject matter. The Celtic names of the main plot were largely given; the Anglo-Saxon names were interpolated with the underplot. The jingling juxtaposition of Edgar and Edmund emphasizes the polarity of the half-brothers. The obsequious Oswald seems to have more than an opening syllable in common with the affected Osric in *Hamlet*. The same repetition imposes a uniformity on three walking gentlemen in *The Merchant of Venice:* Salanio, Salarino, and Salerio. There are only three women in *Coriolanus*, and they are further limited by sharing the same initial: Volumnia, Virgilia, and Valeria. Latin names seem to predominate over Greek even in *Timon of Athens;* yet even in the Greco-Roman sphere of *The Comedy of Errors* there is a Dr. Pinch. The Roman Caius seems to be both a plausible alias for Kent and a suitable patronymic for the French doctor in *The Merry Wives of Windsor*, pronounced like "keys" and doubtless influenced by the Queen's physician of Cambridge fame, Dr. Caius. National terminations are subject to change for metrical reasons: Anthony, Antonio, Antonius. The Latinism Polonius reminds us of the Polish question, moot throughout Hamlet, where the onomastics are polyglot. If Marcellus and Claudius are Latin, Bernardo and Horatio are Italian, and Fortinbras signifies "strong arm" not in Norwegian but French (*fort-en-bras*).

On the other hand, the son of Polonius has a Greek godfather in Laertes, the father of Odysseus. The Scandinavian names, at least the Germanic Gertrude, stand out because they are in the minority. The authentic Norse of the titular name could not have been very meaningful to Shakespeare. Yet it may be the crowning irony that Hamlet, our sobriquet for an intellectual, derives from Amlothi, meaning a simpleton and alluding to the feigned madness of the Prince. Shakespeare manipulates the ironies consciously with Angelo in *Measure for Measure*, who realizes that he is no angel; with Prospero in *The Tempest*, who rounds out a cycle of prosperity and adversity; and with Bianca, the courtesan in *Othello*, who casts her own reflection on the interplay between whiteness and blackness. Failure to live up to one's name results in an anticlimax which Shakespeare coarsely exploits with the clown in *Measure for Measure*, whose first name is Pompey and whose last name is Bum. Like Costard, the clown in *Love's Labour's Lost*, whose name is slang for head, he is imperfect in the role of Pompey the Great; he is, as Costard puts it of himself, "a little o'erparted"; the part is a little too big for him. On a serious level, Shakespeare sometimes found himself constrained by his *donnée,* when the roles had been too often enacted before.

Thus the air of cynical fatalism that hangs over *Troilus and Cressida* is due to the fact that the lovers and their go-between, given their names, could not behave otherwise. Since their names are proverbial, their actions are predestined; for Troilus has already become an eponym: in Rosalind's phraseology, "one of the patterns of love." As Pandarus puts the oath that is foresworn: "Let all constant men be Troiluses, all false women Cressidas, and all brokers-between Pandars!" Since *Troilus and Cressida* contains a hound named Brambler, it is worthy of notice that Petruchio has a spaniel named Troilus, in contradistinction to the English names of the hunting dogs in *The Taming of the Shrew*—or, for that matter, the phantom pack of Ariel in *The Tempest.* There is one hound in both packs which answers to the name of Silver. Unquestionably Launce's Crab in *The Two Gentlemen of Verona* is the greatest scene-stealer among Shakespeare's animals. But the dogs that move us to heartbreak do not exist, except in the delirious imagination of King Lear:

> The little dogs and all,
> Tray, Blanch, and Sweetheart, see, they bark at me.

Shakespeare seems to refer to horses generically, by their condition or breed as in Cut or Roan Barbary.

Such accepted names as Graymalkin for cat and Paddock for toad acquire a grotesque inflection when the Witches invoke them as their familiar spirits.

Through a curiously memorable trick of pseudo-reference, seldom more than the merest passing mention, Shakespeare manages to project a vivid impression of characters who never appear on the stage: poor Robin Ostler, by the road from London to Gadshill, who died when the price of oats rose; Jane Smile, who received the bashful attentions of the youthful Touchstone; Alice Shortcake, who once borrowed a book of riddles from whom but Master Abraham Slender? All our lives are the richer for having heard about them. Mistress Quickly, who has a dubious talent for total recall, peoples the wings with such neighbors: the silkman, Master Smooth; the butcher's wife, Goodwife Keech (keech being a lump of fat); and, less happily, the minister, Master Dumbe, and the deputy, Master Tisick (pthisic?). Sometimes a type is individualized by a courtesy title: *e.g.*, Sir Smile for a hypocrite (*The Winter's Tale*) or Sir Oracle for a pundit (*The Merchant of Venice*)—or, more exotically, Signior Smooth for a flatterer (*Pericles*). The honorific belittles the abstraction when Ulysses deprecates Achilles as Sir Valour or Antonio disposes of Gonzalo as Sir Prudence. Orlando is Signior Love to Jaques, and Jaques is Monsieur Melancholy to Orlando. Benedick's wit transforms Beatrice into Lady Disdain and Claudio into Lord Lackbeard. Falstaff is the target of many such bynames (Monsieur Remorse), and the Host in *The Merry Wives of Windsor* is an expert at devising them (Monsieur Mock-water).

Whenever the cast is prescribed by an anterior plot, it is axiomatic that invention has a freer hand with the lesser parts: Neighbor Mugs, the carrier, for instance, or the shouting tradesmen who follow Jack Cade's rebellion. Servants, wherever they are, have English names more often than not, common enough for the most part but now and then more expressive, like Grindstone and Potpan and the timorous Sampson in *Romeo and Juliet*, where the three musicians vibrate to their stringed instruments: Simon Catling, Hugh Rebeck, and James Soundpost. In the Messina of *Much Ado about Nothing*, where the redoubtable constable and his compartner are Dogberry (the fruit of the dogwood tree) and Verges (rods of office), the stout souls of their watch are Hugh Oatcake and George Seacoal. In the Vienna of *Measure for Measure*, the ultimate guardian of the law is the executioner Abhorson—a portmanteau name with two ill-conditioned compartments, "abhor" and "whoreson." The list of his prisoners is virtually a reckoning of their misdemeanors: Rash, Caper, Stervelackey, Dropheir, Shoetie, Halfcan. Several of Shakespeare's Viennese are recognizable by their un-Austrian charactonyms: Froth, Elbow, Thomas Tapster. Nor should we forget Mistress Overdone, whose profession as bawd would be obvious to contemporaries from the specialized nuance of the verb "to do," and who is more elaborately characterized as Madame Mitigation.

None of Shakespeare's capitals is vaguer or more remote than Pentapolis; yet the shipwrecked Pericles is greeted there by homely fishermen, Patchbreech and Pilch (a crude coat). The names of the Morris-dancing villagers in *The Two Noble Kinsmen* ("Friz and Maudline, And little Luce with the white legs, and bouncing Barbery, And freckled Nell") are about as Athenian as those of the hempen homespuns in *The Midsummer Night's Dream*. When Coriolanus discharges his scorn upon the Roman populace, he specifies them by the commonest of denominators, the nicknames Hob and Dick. Shakespeare can be depended upon to out-English himself upon the home ground of the histories when he is dealing with the little people, like Peter Thump the apprentice, who gives his master a sound thumping in the Second Part of *Henry VI*. But English becomes fully British when Henry V is served by three captains: the Welsh Fluellen, the Irish McMorris, and the Scottish Jamy. On the eve of the Battle of Agincourt, Shakespeare envisions

A little touch of Harry in the night,

when the King fraternizes on the battlefield with three common soldiers: John Bates, Alexander Court, and Michael Williams. He goes incognito as "Harry Leroy," which Pistol thinks must be a Cornish name. As the language expresses an upsurging patriotism, so the names assert an underlying democracy. King Henry, when he was plain Prince Hal, had learned to drink with the good lads of Eastcheap and to "call them all by their christen names, as Tom, Dick, and Francis." We might have expected a Harry to be the third in that convivial trio; but Francis was the tavern boy with whom the Prince had been jesting; and Tilley's *Dictionary of Sixteenth-Century Proverbs* makes clear that "Tom, Dick, and Harry" was not yet the standard expression for indiscriminate camaraderie. Shakespeare may have helped to crystallize it with his King Harry.

The popularity of the royal nickname was confirmed by the Tudors; Henry VII and Henry VIII were linked with the most popular of the Lancaster Henries, the former Prince Hal. Whereas King Henry IV is referred to as Bolingbroke from the name of his castle, the Prince of Wales was Harry Monmouth from his birthplace in Wales, and was therewith differentiated from his heroic rival, Harry Percy, surnamed Hotspur for his splenetic valor. It is even fancied, by Henry Bolingbroke, that those two younger Harries might have been exchanged in their cradles. Ultimately they must fight it out in an alliterative duel to the death:

> Harry to Harry shall, hot horse to horse,
> Meet and ne'er part till one fall down a corse.

It was predictable that the victorious Harry would wed a woman whom he could address by that most Shakespearean of feminine nicknames, Kate. She is the French Princess Catherine, of course; but Petruchio insists on making a Kate out of his Italian Katherina, despite her emphatic objections. Katherine of Aragon may retain her formal dignity; but the other Harry, Hotspur, has a wife who is rechristened Kate by Shakespeare—even though, historically speaking, Lady Percy's maiden name was Elizabeth (Mortimer). Shakespeare's heroes are fond of punning on "cates," meaning delicacies; some of them imply a less flattering jingle on "cats," meaning prostitutes. Of such is Kate Keepdown in *Measure for Measure*, or the tailor's Kate to whom the sailors preferred Moll, Meg, Marian, and Margery in the sea chanty of *The Tempest*.

Nell is not much less basic, as applied to the Duchess Eleanor in the Second Part of *Henry VI* or—most informally—to Helen of Troy by Paris in *Troilus and Cressida*. It seems more suitable for the offstage slattern described by the out-of-town Dromio in *The Comedy of Errors*. Yet the hostess, Mistress Quickly, who appears to be an Ursula in the Second Part of *Henry IV*, somehow becomes a Nell in *Henry V*. She has become a more respectable figure to us, as the advance of years has muffled the pun on "quick-lie." Nor, while we are citing occupational names, should we overlook her friend and protégée, Doll Tearsheet. Coleridge, who was constantly trying to purify Shakespeare's mind, tried to emend the metonym to Tearstreet. It is a far cry, which demonstrates Shakespeare's range, to the innocent wide-eyed girls of the later romances with their lyrical names: Marina, child of the sea, in *Pericles;* Perdita, the lost one, in *The Winter's Tale;* and the wondrous and wondering, the admiring and admirable Miranda of *The Tempest.* In contrast with their poetic remoteness, nothing could be simpler or more downright than plain Joan. When the Bastard Faulconbridge is dubbed by King John, he declares:

> Well, now can I make any Joan a lady.

And when Beroune confesses his love and denounces his luck, in *Love's Labour's Lost,* he repeats the antithesis:

> Some men must love my lady, and some Joan.

And in the refrain of the song that closes the play, as the elegant French ladies are departing, we are accorded a glimpse of that rustic creature, "greasy Joan," stirring the pot at a wintry hearth. These simplicities may have some bearing on Shakespeare's reductive attitude toward Joan of Arc.

Nor does he hesitate to draw upon folklore, while he is exemplifying the way of a maid with a man: of Tib with Tom or of Jill with Jack. Jack appears ordinarily as a term of contempt; but for us it has the friendliest connotations; for we cannot but associate it with "Jack Falstaff to his familiars, John to his brothers and sisters, and Sir John to all Europe." Here we encounter a coinage brightly minted by genius in the matrix of circumstance. We are aware that Shakespeare's supreme comic figure was originally known as Sir John Oldcastle, after a historic personage, indeed an unseasonably austere Protestant leader, and that Shakespeare—apparently responding to a Puritan protest—saw fit to withdraw the allusion and to hint an apology in the epilogue to the Second Part of *Henry IV*. The substitution has no exact counterpart anywhere, but it does recall Sir John Fastolfe, who is reported to have played the coward in the First Part of *King Henry VI*. Furthermore the metathesis, from Fastolfe to Falstaff, has an enlarging significance. A writer named Shakespeare, whose contemporaries jested about his name and whose incomparable sensitivity to words might have been intensified for that reason, must have been quite conscious of what he was doing when he renamed his fat knight Falstaff. *Shake spear ..... Fall staff*. A metaphorical staff is flourished and dropped at Gadshill, Eastcheap, and Shrewsbury. Just as Cleopatra mourns, "The soldier's pole is fall'n," so "Falstaff" accentuates the mock-heroic theme.

His raffish subalterns are calculated to fit in well with it: Pistol, who is so noisily self-explanatory; Peto, who may have something to do with *petard* and its uncouth etymology; Nym, who conforms to his synonym for filch; Gadshill, who picked up his alias at the scene of the highway robbery; and Bardolph, who seems to have pinched his from Lord Bardolph. Bardolph's ragged conscripts rate an honorable listing in the chronicles of realism: Ralph Mouldy, Simon Shadow, Thomas Wart, Francis Feeble, and Peter

Bullcalf. Perhaps the most remarkable *tour de force* is the evocation of personalities not simply absent but long dead, through the nostalgic recollections of Justice Shallow. These, we gather from Falstaff (who at first mistakes his name for Master Surecard), are much livelier than his youthful escapades ever were: swaggering at the Inns of Court with Francis Pickbone and Will Squele, a Cotswold man (Shakespeare's Williams tend to be slightly comic); fighting with one Sampson Stockfish, who—oddly enough—seems to have been a fruiterer, not a fishmonger; and teasing that *bona roba*, Jane Nightwork, who had Robin Nightwork by old Nightwork some fifty-five years ago. Robert Shallow, Esquire, for all his name, adds a dimension with his reminiscence. Yet the fondest of memories fade. Not long afterward Mistress Page cannot hit upon Falstaff's name, and even the conscientious Fluellen has forgotten it. Would they have remembered Oldcastle, we wonder?

Shakespeare's overt fools—above all, Touchstone —bear names as sententious as they are. Yet the profoundest of them, like the unnameable spokesman of Samuel Beckett, is the nameless fool of *King Lear*. The quarto text of *Love's Labour's Lost* has a way of introducing characters as if they were types in the *commedia dell'arte*, referring to the Braggart for Don Armado and to the Pedant for Holofernes. Shakespeare particularizes by naming his Spaniard for the vainglorious Armada and his schoolmaster for Gargantua's tutor in Rabelais. In the universe of the pedantic Holofernes, everything has its appopriate label. Why was Ovid's family name identical with the Latin word for nose? "And why indeed Naso but for smelling out the odoriferous flowers of fancy, the jerks of invention?" Life is not always so ingeniously tagged by literature; that is one of the points scored by *Love's Labour's Lost*. Yet man's command over his environment hinges upon that faculty exerted by Adam and Eve when they named the beasts in the garden, or by Prospero when he endowed Caliban's purposes with words, and taught him how to tell the sun from the moon,

> how
> To name the bigger light, and how the less,
> That burn by day, and night.

Caliban, whose name is an imperfect anagram of *cannibal*, making mischief with the sodden Stefano and with Trinculo, whose name is a clinking toast, cannot be considered an apt pupil. But through the ministrations of Ariel, whose name betokens his ethereal flights, and through the consequent magic of Prospero's art, Shakespeare conjures and creates with words. It is no mere superstition that prompts Glendower to reinforce his authority by reckoning up the names of the several devils—devils whom mine Host of the Garter swears by, and against whose torments Edgar cries out. Their demonic potency, figuratively construed, is nothing less than the control of nature. For the power of naming is intimately allied to the gift of characterization.

And as imagination bodies forth
The forms of things unknown, the poet's pen
Turns them to shapes, and gives to airy nothing
A local habitation and a name.

"With That Facility":

False Starts and Revisions in
Love's Labour's Lost

BY J. V. CUNNINGHAM

THE title-page of the earliest extant edition of
Love's Labour's Lost, the First Quarto of 1598,
describes the play as "A Pleasant Conceited
Comedie." [1] This is, of course, an advertisement, a
blurb, and indeed we know from various allusions that
title-pages were struck off separately and displayed
"at the recognised 'posts' throughout the town" "to
catch a termer." [2] But an advertisement tells us something: it tells us what a seller thinks will be attractive
to a buyer, and what it says of a product may sometimes be so. It is, I think, so in this instance. What is it
a prospective buyer would anticipate who was inter-

[1] *Love's Labour's Lost, 1598.* Shakespeare Quarto Facsimiles, No.
10 (Oxford, 1957). All quotations are from this text.
[2] R. B. McKerrow in *Shakespeare's England* (Oxford, 1932), II,
231. Thomas Campion, *Works*, ed. Percival Vivian (Oxford, 1909),
p. 34.

ested in a pleasant conceited comedy? The description is not uncommon on the title-pages of that time, though not routine. We have "The Old Wives Tale, a pleasant conceited Comedie . . ." in 1595; "A Pleasant Conceited Historie, called The taming of a shrew" in 1594; and the earliest text of *Romeo and Juliet,* the Bad Quarto of 1597, is "An Excellent conceited Tragedie. . . ." The term "conceit," of course, was also used to describe the striking hi-jinks of a comic character; the First Quarto of *1 Henry IV,* for example, promises on the title-page, not only the Battle of Shrewsbury, but also "the humorous conceits of Sir John Falstaffe." [3] But when applied to a play as a whole, whether comedy, tragedy, or history, though it is peculiarly appropriate to comedy, "conceited" indicates that the work will be especially rhetorical in style, full of witty and ingenious turns of thought and speech.

It is interesting that whatever reputation Shakespeare had in the literary and theatrical world of London up to 1598, so far as we can recover it from the records of the time, was not a reputation for creation of character or contrivance of plot but precisely for qualities of style, and particularly for pleasant, conceited writing. The evidence is, considering the scantiness of records of this sort, surprisingly full. The first clear reference linking Shakespeare and the stage

[3] E. K. Chambers, *The Elizabethan Stage* (Oxford, 1923), III, 461; IV, 48; III, 483, 485.

is, of course, the allusion by Greene in a pamphlet of
1592 to Shakespeare as player turned playwright; an
antic, Greene says, "garnisht in our colours," that is,
ornamented in those colors of rhetoric, those figures
of speech, which the writer gives to the actor, and yet
he now thinks "he is as well able to bombast out a
blanke verse as the best of" the professional play-
wrights: that is, to fill out "the spacious volubilitie of a
drumming decasillabon," no doubt with "farre-fetcht
phraise," for bombast, of course, is the foam rubber of
the time, the material used to pad out fashionable
clothing. Shakespeare, a mere actor, has picked up
Greene's style and meter, the new style and meter that
made possible the glories of the late Elizabethan stage.
Chettle in a subsequent apology for Greene's attack,
also of 1592, speaks particularly of Shakespeare's
"facetious grace in writting, that approues his Art";
that is, to translate the compliment into modern idiom,
the witty and ingenious charm of style that ratifies his
skill. For Barnfield in 1598 it is Shakespeare's "hony-
flowing Vaine," his mastery of the sweet style, that
pleases the world and praise obtains. In the well-
known catalogues of Francis Meres, also of 1598,
Shakespeare is listed with his peers, Sidney, Spenser,
and others, as one by whom "The English tongue is
mightiliy enriched, and gorgeouslie inuested in rare
ornaments and resplendent abiliments"; again, "the
Muses would speak with Shakespeares fine filed
phrase, if they would speake English"; and, finally,

"the sweete wittie soule of Ouid liues in mellifluous &
hony-tongued *Shakespeare*." [4]

One would expect, then, from the promise of the
title-page and from the reputation of the author, that
Love's Labour's Lost would be a work replete with
witty, charming, ingenious turns of thought and
speech, that it would be a display of the rhetoric of
the sweet, the pleasant style, the *genus amoenum* of
Antiquity. And so it is.

It is, in fact, so much of a display that, when the
reader or viewer comes to the middle of the last scene,
he will be suddenly delighted and relieved. For there
the hero of the play renounces his rhetoric:

> O neuer will I trust to speaches pend,
> Nor to the motion of a Schoole-boyes tongue:
> Nor neuer come in vizard to my friend,
> Nor woo in rime like a blind harpers songue.
> Taffata phrases, silken tearmes precise,
> Three pilde Hiberboles, spruce affection:
> Figures pedanticall, these sommer flies,
> Haue blowne me full of maggot ostentation.
> I do forsweare them. . . . (5.2. 402–10)

The modern lover, whose eloquence is confined to re-
citing what he takes to be the story of his life and who

---

[4] E. K. Chambers, *William Shakespeare: A Study of Facts and
Problems* (Oxford, 1930), II, 188. Thomas Nashe, "Preface to
Menaphon," *Works*, ed. R. B. McKerrow (Oxford, 1958), III, 312.
The Collected Poems of Joseph Hall, ed. A. Davenport (Liverpool,
1949), p. 16. Chambers, *Shakespeare*, II, 189, 195, 194.

demands of love the illusions of sincerity, feels now at home. He applauds as Berowne goes on:

and I here protest
By this white Gloue (how white the
hand God knowes)
Hencefoorth my wooing minde shalbe exprest
In russet yeas, and honest kersie noes.

And does not notice that Berowne, in renouncing rhetoric, renounces it rhetorically, crowding in one phrase the figures of exclamation, asseveration, and one of the varieties of verbal repetition. He cannot renounce it, for to speak in russet and kersey would be inappropriate to his rank in society and to Rosaline's, and inappropriate to courtly love. For russet and kersey are cheap cloths, the dress of the lowborn, and one woos only the lowborn in russet yeas and honest kersey noes. Thus, when Don Armado of the fantastic phrase woos Jacquenetta, the country wench, he says with absolute russet simplicity:
"Maide."
To which Jacquenetta replies in kersey:
"Man."

But the play deals chiefly with love at court and courtly love, and both demand witty invention and figurative language. For, as an elder contemporary of Shakespeare's tells us: "But as it hath bene always reputed a great fault to vse figuratiue speaches foolishly and indiscretly, so it is esteemed no lesse an imperfection in mans vtterance, to haue none vse of figure at all, specially in our writing and speaches publike, making them but as our ordinary talke. . . ." To make the point clear he uses the very analogy that the hero used above, and that Francis Meres used in the passage alluded to earlier where he spoke of the English tongue "gorgeouslie inuested in rare ornaments and resplendent abiliments": "And as we see in these great Madames of honour, be they for personage or otherwise neuer so comely and bewtifull, yet if they want their courtly habilements or at leastwise such other apparell as custome and ciuilitie haue ordained to couer their naked bodies, would be halfe ashamed or greatly out of countenaunce to be seen in that sort, and perchance do then thinke themselves more amiable in euery mans eye, when they be in their richest attire, suppose of silkes or tyssewes & costly embroideries, then when they go in cloth or in any other plaine and simple apparell. Even so cannot our vulgar Poesie shew it selfe either gallant or gorgious, if any lymme be left naked and bare and not clad in his kindly clothes and coulours, such as may conuey them some what out of sight, that is from the common course of ordinary speach and capacitie of the vulgar iudgement. . . ."

Style, then, is an ornament, and a needed ornament, but it must also be fitting and proper. And what is fitting and proper to love at court? Or, to quote our author again, "In what forme of poesie the amorous affections and allurements were uttered." He answers: "And because loue is of all other humane affections the most puissant and passionate . . . it requireth a forme of poesie variable, inconstant, affected, curious, and most witty of any others. . . ."[5] "Variable," "inconstant," "affected," "curious," and "most witty" —the terms need explanation since, except perhaps for the last, they do not at all mean what the modern reader would take them to mean. It must be "variable," that is, there should be a copious variety of phrases, a flow and outpouring of eloquence, such as we shall see later in Berowne's display, making the worse appear the better cause. It should be "inconstant"; the style should not keep a single tenor, but rise and fall, with a mingling of styles. The violation of these two requirements in his own sonnets is the theme of Shakespeare's seventy-sixth sonnet:

Why is my verse so barren of new pride?
So far from variation or quicke change?

The style should also be "affected"; that is, it should show feeling. It should be "curious," or carefully, highly, finely wrought, and "most witty," with many turns and conceits of speech and thought.

It is an old theory of style, though out of fashion in our day, and clearly relevant to *Love's Labour's Lost*. The play as a whole is an illustration of the qualities of style of amorous poesy, as also at times of the foolish and indiscreet use of figurative speeches. The theory was simple: it distinguished between the naked thought nakedly expressed and the same thought de-

---

[5] *The Arte of English Poesie* (London, 1589), STC microfilm, Reel 421: 3.2., p. 115, Q4r; 3.1., pp. 314–15; 1.22, p. 36, G2v.

cently or even gorgeously apparelled. The problem in practice was to achieve, first, an ability to clothe any thought in rich and varied costume, to have "a mint of phrases in his braine" (1.1.166); and then to exercise discretion in choosing just what was suited to this speaker, addressing this person, on this occasion. The prior problem, of course, though usually subsequent in attainment, was to find the thought. They called this "invention," borrowing the Latin word for finding, and they especially prized an invention that was apt and peculiarly fitted to the speaker, audience, and circumstances.

Such was the theory and practice of composition in Shakespeare's day. That he wrote explicitly by it, at least at times, is clear from several passages in this play. These are passages where, with some uncertainty but also with a good deal of plausibility, we can see Shakespeare at work.

But perhaps we should dwell for a moment on this point, for the desire to find genius at work has sometimes dispensed with scrutiny of the evidence. There have been those, and there still are, who would like to see in, for example, the earliest printed texts of *Romeo and Juliet* and *Hamlet,* the Bad Quartos as they are called in modern scholarship, Shakespearean first drafts, or the inferior work of a Shakespearean predecessor, or, most commonly, some mingling of both early draft and other work. The critic can then show by comparison how the prior effort has been transformed into a Shakespearean masterpiece. But if the current view of most textual critics is correct, the process is the other way around, and the evidence is no evidence for Shakespeare at work. It is not that a prior effort has been transformed by Shakespeare, but that Shakespeare has been mercilessly transformed and corrupted by others. For there is fairly general agreement that the Bad Quartos are reconstructions from memory of the authentic text. Why it was done, and by whom, are subjects for conjecture and imaginative fiction. But surely the "To be or not to be" soliloquy in its first published form would require a more than Shakespearean genius to transform it into the form we know. It reads:

> To be, or not to be, I there's the point,
> To Die, to sleepe, is that all? I all:
> No, to sleepe, to dreame, I mary there it goes,
> For in that dreame of death, when wee awake,
> And borne before an euerlasting Judge,
> From whence no passenger euer retur'nd,
> The vndiscouered country, at whose sight
> The happy smile, and the accursed damn'd.

And so on, for fourteen more lines.

There is in the portion I have just read something that does tend to support the view that this version represents an effort to remember and record the received text:

> To Die, to sleepe, is that all? I all:
> No, to sleepe, to dreame, I mary there it goes.

The man who is trying to remember the speech is dictating to a secretary who writes down all, including "No, that's not the way it goes," and "Yes, yes, that's the way it goes."

But the texts we will deal with and the evidence for revision are of a different kind, for we will be concerned with passages where the earliest editions preserve in the same text alternate versions of the same speech. It is not a situation peculiar to *Love's Labour's Lost;* there are other instances. In *Othello,* for one, there is a passage (2.1.77–83) whose significance for the textual history of the play has not been appraised. There are two early editions, the Quarto of 1622, and the Folio of 1623. The passage reads in the Quarto:

—great *Iove Othello* guard,
And swell his saile with thine owne powerfull breath,
That he may blesse this Bay with his tall shippe,
And swiftly come to *Desdemona's* armes.
 Enter Desdemona, Iago, Emillia, *and* Roderigo.
Give renewd fire,
To our extincted spirits.
And bring all Cypresse comfort,—O behold
The riches of the ship is come ashore.

In the Folio:

Great Ioue, *Othello* guard,
And swell his Saile with thine owne powrefull breath,
That he may blesse this Bay with his tall Ship,
Make loues quicke pants in *Desdemonaes* Armes,

Give renew'd fire to our extincted Spirits.
　　Enter Desdemona, Iago, Rodorigo, and Aemilia.
Oh, behold,
The Riches of the Ship is come on shore:

The texts are substantially identical up to line 80. There the author wrote "And swiftly come to Desdemona's arms," bringing the sentence and the speech to a close. Then, for whatever reasons, and I think we can see plausible reasons, he crossed out "And swiftly come," interlined "Make loues quicke pants," and swung the sentence over the line-end, making more vivid Othello's private life and acknowledging his public role.

What is textually interesting here is that one needs both Quarto and Folio to recover what Shakespeare wrote and what he rejected; that is, there must have been a manuscript ultimately common to both texts in which both first draft and revision indistinguishably stood. It would in this respect be like the copy for Romeo's last speech in the Good Quarto of 1599. The relevant portion reads:

　　Ah deare *Iuliet*
why art thou yet so faire? I will beleeve,
Shall I beleeve that vnsubstantiall death is amorous,
And that the leane abhorred monster keepes
Thee here in the darke to be his parramour?
For feare of that I still will staie with thee,
And never from this pallat of dym night.
Depart againe, come lye thou in my arme,

Heer's to thy health, where ere thou tumblest in.
O true Appothecarie!
Thy drugs are quicke. Thus with a kisse I die.
Depart againe, here, here, will I remaine,
With wormes that are thy Chamber-maides: O here
Will I set up my everlasting rest:
And shake the yoke of inauspicious starres,
From this world wearied flesh, eyes looke your last:
Armes take your last embrace: And lips, O you
The doores of breath, seale with a righteous kisse
A dateless bargaine to ingrossing death:
Come bitter conduct, come vnsauory guide,
Thou desperate Pilot, now at once run on
The dashing Rocks, thy seasick weary barke:
Heeres to my Love. O true Appothecary:
Thy drugs are quicke. Thus with a kisse I die.

There are two false starts in the passage, both lov-
ingly preserved by the printer, and both, of course,
cancelled by the subsequent revision. And we can,
given the evidence, see why. This is Romeo's great
aria, and so the declarative "I will beleeve" is immediately altered to the heightened form of a rhetorical
question. What follows is adequate, but not suffi-
ciently extended, not copious enough, and not suffi-
ciently elevated; indeed, with "where ere thou tumblest in" it falls to vulgarity. And so Shakespeare picks
up "Depart againe," getting thirteen lines for four,
introducing a Gorgianic figure of the vultures-are-
living-sepulchres type ("With wormes that are thy

Chamber-maides"), figures of verbal repetition ("here, here," "O here"), apostrophe, personification ("Come bitter conduct"), periphrasis ("And lips, O you/ The doores of breath")—a speech variable, inconstant, affected, curious, and in an Elizabethan sense most witty.

The passages in *Love's Labour's Lost* are similar to the *Romeo* passage. We have the first draft and the revision, and we can see what was done to it. In each case the revised version immediately follows the first draft, and in two cases repeats with slight variation the opening line of the first draft. An eighteenth-century editor who first noted one of these passages (4.3.291ff.) explained convincingly what had happened in that instance: "penned in haste, found weak in some places, and its reasoning disjointed, it had instant correction; but wanting the proper mark of correction by rasure or otherwise, printers took what they found." [6]

There are three such passages, two of which have been noticed by previous commentators. But the third is the simplest, and we will begin with that. It reads in the earliest extant edition, 1598 (the Pedant, Holofernes, is speaking):

Peda. Sir, you shall present before her the Nine Worthies. Sir *Holofernes*, as concerning some entertainement of time, some show in the posterior of this

[6] Capell in Variorum (Philadelphia, n.d.), 4th impression, ad 4.3.317–322 and 330–338, p. 193.

day, to be rended by our assistants the Kinges commaund, and this most gallant illustrate and learned Gentleman, before the Princesse: I say none so fit as to present the nine Worthies. (5.1.124–30)

There is a minor point to be noted in this passage before we come to the major one. The passage is reprinted in the first collected edition of Shakespeare's plays, 1623, with one correction: "rendered" for "rended." This could be right, for certainly the Pedant intended to say "rendered." But it is more likely that Shakespeare intended him to mistake the word and say "rended" instead. For the rendering of the Nine Worthies, when we come to it a little later, is certainly "rended," limb from limb. It is a habit of Shakespeare's comic characters to say the unselfconsciously obvious thing, to "mistake the word" [7] to their own derogation. For instance, the clown says in this play of a letter, "Sir the contempts thereof are as touching me" (1.1.191).

We come now to the major point. The Pedant, of course, is Holofernes, and so he would seem in the second sentence to be addressing himself. This is obviously wrong. One could perhaps justify it by some exquisite psychological construction but such subtlety would be out of place in a broadly comic speech. Besides, the Pedant is not entitled to be called "Sir," and Elizabethans were very finicky on such details. On the other hand, Nathaniel, the Curate, is entitled to "Sir"

[7] TGV, 3.1.283.

by virtue of his office, and editors usually correct "Holofernes" to "Nathaniel," so that the first sentence is addressed in direct reply to Armado, the second to Sir Nathaniel. But this is clumsy. Furthermore, both sentences say exactly the same thing, the first straightforwardly, the second in the Pedant's own style. The first is the naked thought; the second is clothed in figures pedantical.

The traces of what happened are clear on the printed page. Shakespeare wrote the speech prefix "Peda." and put down in a straightforward sentence what he wanted him to say. Then, perhaps after a warm beer, he started over, writing the speech prefix "Holofernes," and recast what he wanted him to say in pedantical style. Either he neglected to mark the first sentence for deletion or the printer missed the mark. In the second sentence the printer corrected "Holofernes Sir" to the more plausible "Sir Holofernes." If this reconstruction is correct the passage should begin:

> *Holofernes.* Sir, as concerning some
> entertainement . . .

And how does Shakespeare go about recasting the original sentence? First, he turns it into a suspended, a periodic sentence, sending out an extended flanker movement before bringing up the main clause. This tends to elevation of style, and recognizes the social gulf between Armado, who is addressed, and the Pedant. Second, the notion in "you shall present" is expanded into two phrases, the second employing the phrase he had a moment before collected for his own phrase-book from Armado's jewelled speech: "The *posterior* of the day, most generous sir, is liable, congruent, and measurable for the after noone: the worde is well culd, chose, sweete, & apt I do assure you sir, I do assure." And finally, he finds a Latinate, an aureate term, "illustrate," to go with the other two complimentary epithets by which Armado is addressed. It is like "peregrinate," earlier in the scene, which Sir Nathaniel wrote down in his notebook for future use, "A most singuler and choyce Epithat."

The second passage comes towards the end of the last scene of the play. The princess has imposed a year's penance on the king, at the end of which he may claim her in marriage. After this, in the earliest edition, Berowne says to Rosaline, "And what to me my Loue? and what to me?" And she replies:

You must be purged to, your sinnes are rackt.
You are attaint with faultes and periurie:
Therefore if you my fauour meane to get,
A tweluemonth shall you spende and neuer rest,
But seeke the weery beddes of people sicke.

(5.2.827-32)

Whereupon Dumaine says to Katherine, almost echoing the words of Berowne, "But what to me my Loue? but what to me?" And after she has put him off for a year, and Maria has put Longaville off for the same period, Berowne again addresses Rosaline, and

she again imposes the same sentence on him, but with
a significant addition:

> Oft haue I heard of you my Lord *Berowne*,
> Before I saw you: and the worldes large tongue
> Proclaymes you for a man repleat with mockes,
> Full of comparisons and wounding floutes:
> Which you on all estetes will execute,
> That lie within the mercie of your wit:
> To weede this wormewood from your
>   fructfull braine,
> And therewithal to winne me, yf you please,
> Without the which I am not to be won:
> You shall this tweluemonth terme from day to day,
> Visite the speachless sicke, and still conuerse,
> With groning wretches: and your taske shall be,
> With all the fierce endeuour of your wit,
> To enforce the pained impotent to smile. (851–64)

It is generally agreed that here too the printer set up
an unrevised version followed by the revised version.
In writing this final scene Shakspeare knew that by all
laws of precedence the king's exchange with the princess must come first. He then went on with Berowne
and Rosaline, who perhaps interested him as they interest us, but soon saw that by all the laws of interest
these two must come last. So he started over, gave
Berowne's speech to Dumaine with the change of
"And" to "But," and after taking care of the other
lovers returned to the hero and heroine. He must have
seen that Rosaline's original speech was not only

much too short for the purpose but also pretty flat in the writing. Furthermore, the penance imposed on the hero had no special ingenuity to it, no exact fitting of the punishment to the crime. What he needs, then, is a notion, a gimmick, an invention, and this will yield the detail to amplify the passage and give it the requisite bulk. He keeps, then, only the idea of "purged" and develops it in the line "To weede this wormewood from your fructfull braine."

And for penance? Berowne's sin has been wit. He has been

> a man repleat with mockes,
> Full of comparisons and wounding floutes:
> Which you on all estetes will execute,
> That lie within the mercie of your wit.

And so the original idea of sentencing him to tending the sick for twelve months is given an apt and decorous twist:

> You shall this tweluemonth terme from day to day,
> Visite the speachless sicke, and still conuerse,
> With groaning wretches: and your taske shall be,
> With all the fierce endeuour of your wit,
> To enforce the pained impotent to smile.

The description of Berowne as a wit and the description of his penitential expense of that wit furnish the material for amplification.

In the first passage we found Shakespeare writing down what he wanted to say, and then saying it as he wanted to say it. The problem is one of clothing the thought. In the second passage the proper management of the ending led him to cancel the lines, and the flatness of style and of the climactic idea forced him to develop new lines and an ingenious twist of the old idea. It was a question of invention.

The third passage is the most extensive, and the one in which the reconstruction of the process of composition is the most conjectural. This is the first draft;

Haue at you then affections men at armes,
Consider what you first did sweare vnto:
To fast, to study, and to see no woman:
Flat treason gainst the kingly state of youth.
Say, Can you fast? your stomacks are too young:
And abstinence ingenders maladies.
And where that you haue vowd to Studie (Lordes)
In that each of you haue forsworne his Booke.
Can you still dreame and poare and thereon looke.
For when would you my Lord, or you, or you,
Haue found the ground of Studies excellence,
Without the beautie of a womans face?
From womens eyes this doctrine I deriue,
They are the Ground, the Bookes, the Achadems,
From whence doth spring the true *Promethean* fire.
Why vniuerfall plodding poysons vp
The nimble spirites in the arteries,
As motion and long during action tyres
The sinnowy vigour of the trauayler.
Now for not looking on a womans face,

You haue in that forsworne the vse of eyes:
And studie too, the causer of your vow.
For where is any Authour in the worlde,
Teaches such beautie as a womans eye:
Learning is but an adiunct to our selfe,
And where we are, our Learning likewise is.
Then when our selues we see in Ladies eyes,
With our selues.
Do we not likewise see our learning there?

(4.3.291-318)

There is no question of invention here. Berowne has already used at the beginning of the play (1.1.59ff.) the line of argument by which he will make the worse appear the better cause, and used it in a similar context. It is an extemporal display of wit, like the display of a fencing master: "Com'on then" in the earlier passage, and "Haue at you then" here. And it employs the same commonplace of the vanity of learning: "continuall plodders" in the first act, and "vniuersall plodding" here. It is a display in the tradition of Nashe, and perhaps of Tarleton: "but giue me the man whose extemporall veine in any humour will excell our greatest Art-maisters deliberate thoughts; whose inuentions, quicker than his eye, will challenge the prowdest Rhetoritian to the contention of like perfection with like expedition." [8]

There are some indications at the beginning and end of this first draft that Shakespeare was getting down

[8] Nashe, *Works*, III, 312.

something to say, as he did in the Holofernes passage. The line, "In that each of you haue forsworne his Booke," lacks metrical and rhetorical shape; it is a line that belongs to another style, a consequence of rhetorically unsuccessful exactness. In the next line he overcorrects by introducing rhyme in a line that is too easily and obviously shaped: "Can you still dreame and poare and thereon looke." There is a similar unsuccessful exactness at the end of the passage where he is trying out a new line of argument. Here the separate line "With our selues" has puzzled editors, and they have tended simply to omit it. But the argument is drawn from metaphysics—it is a development of the proposition "Learning is but an adiunct to our selfe" —and Shakespeare is trying to get it down exactly. He wrote, "Then when our selues we see in Ladies eyes, with our selues do we not likewise see our learning there?" He moved from verse to the exactness of prose; it was more reason than rhyme. But since metrical composition involves a habit of forming sentences simultaneously grammatical and metrical, the last ten syllables come in a syntactical unit metrically acceptable, and the printer set it up as verse. At this point Shakespeare abandons the thought, and the first start, and starts over again:

O we haue made a Vow to studie, Lordes,
And in that Vow we haue forsworne our Bookes:
For when would you (my Leedge) or you, or you?
In leaden contemplation haue found out

Such fierie Numbers as the prompting eyes,
Of beautis tutors haue inritcht you with:
Other slow Artes intirely keepe the braine:
And therefore finding barraine practizers,
Scarce shew a haruest of their heauie toyle.
But Loue first learned in a Ladies eyes,
Liues not alone emured in the braine:
But with the motion of all elamentes,
Courses as swift as thought in euery power,
And giues to euery power a double power,
Aboue their functions and their offices.
It addes a precious seeing to the eye:
A Louers eyes will gaze an Eagle blinde.
A Louers eare will heare the lowest sound,
When the suspitious head of theft is stopt.
Loues feeling is more soft and sensible,
Then are the tender hornes of Cockled Snayles.
Loues tongue proues daintie, *Bachus* grosse in taste,
For Valoure, is not Loue a *Hercules?*
Still clyming trees in the *Hesperides.*
Subtit as *Sphinx,* as sweete and musicall,
As bright *Appolos* Lute, strung with his haire.
And when Loue speakes, the voyce of all the Goddes,
Make heauen drowsie with the harmonie.
Neuer durst Poet touch a pen to write,
Vntill his Incke were tempred with Loues sighes:
O then his lines would rauish sauage eares,
And plant in Tyrants milde humilitie.
From womens eyes this doctrine I deriue,
They sparcle still the right promethean fier,

They are the bookes, the Arts, the Achademes,
That shew, containe, and nourish all the worlde.
Els none at all in ought proues excellent.
Then fooles you were, these women to forsweare:
Or keeping what is sworne, you will proue fooles,
For Wisedomes sake, a worde that all men loue:
Or for Loues sake, a worde that loues all men.
Or for Mens sake, the authour of these Women:
Or Womens sake, by whom we Men are Men.
Let vs once loose our othes to finde our selues,
Or els we loose our selues, to keepe our othes:
It is Religion to be thus forsworne.
For Charitie it selfe fulfilles the Law:
And who can seuer Loue from Charitie. (4.3.318-65)

Shakespeare had two problems, a problem of order
and of amplification; the speech had to have size and
to move. He had begun in the earlier wit display by
dividing his subject; he will take up the three vows in
order. But the line of argument is that the second
vow, "to study," entails rejection of the third vow,
"to see no woman," and hence part three of the
speech, which is clearly indicated by the transitional
"now for not looking on a womans face," must in
effect simply repeat in other words the content of
part two. He needs, then, a new principle of order,
and suddenly finds it. He fuses the two vows, treats
them together as inherently they demand to be
treated, and fuses at the same time much of the detail
of the draft. The notion of women as teachers be-

comes "beauty's tutors" who teach love poetry. The earlier "vniversal plodding" suggests "leaden contemplation," as also the distinction of "Other slow arts." Out of the same sentence, dropping the inapt simile of the traveller, he picks up the physiological notion of "The nimble spirites in the arteries," which perform in Elizabethan science the functions of our modern "nervous system"; this is now identified with love, which "Courses as swift as thought in euery power" and increases each faculty. He proceeds to amplify, as the textbooks suggest he should, by division. The five senses are faculties, and so he enumerates four of them.

And why not five? Partly because the fifth would complete a pattern and might bring the fluent facility to a stop, and partly because he has suddenly found another principle of order that will keep the eloquence flowing. He will now move from new material to new material by clear and simple associative links. "Love's tongue proues daintie, *Bachus* grosse in taste" suggests a richer field of amplification, mythological comparisons, culminating in "the voyce of all the Goddes." This suggests poetry and the effects of music. When this flags, he has at hand the salvaged lines on the true Promethean fire, and brings the argument to a conclusion, summarizing in a pointed couplet:

Then fooles you were, these women to forsweare:
Or keeping what is sworne, you will proue fooles.

But the impetus persists; he is not willing to quit. The pointed couplet with its repetitions suggests a passage of verbal repetition: for, as a contemporary says, "the eares of men are not onlie delighted with store & exchange of divers words, but feele greate delight in repeticion of the same. . . ." [9] And now he finally concludes with what is really conclusive, and plucked out of nowhere, a Scriptural text: "For Charitie it selfe fulfilles the Law."

One sympathizes with the judgment of his colleague, Ben Jonson: "Hee . . . had an excellent *Phantsie;* brave notions, and gentle expressions: wherein hee flow'd with that facility, that sometimes it was necessary he should be stop'd. . . . His wit was in his owne power; would the rule of it had been so too." [10]

[9] Louise Brown Osborn, *The Life, Letters, and Writings of John Hoskyns* (New Haven, 1937), p. 125.
[10] *Works,* ed. Herford, Simpson, and Simpson (Oxford, 1925–1952), VIII, 584.

Judgment in *Hamlet*

BY GUNNAR BOKLUND

ONE of the best testimonies to Shakespeare's enduring popularity is provided by the abundance and variety of the literature on *Hamlet*. No sensible critic hopes to say the last word on the subject or even to influence the taste of his generation to any appreciable extent. He tries to make a contribution to our understanding of a complex play, either by analyzing some frequently overlooked aspect of it, on which his special knowledge can be brought to bear, or by presenting his reading of the whole tragedy, the way in which a presumably intelligent and well-informed individual reacts to it. The character of Prince Hamlet has always been at the center of interest, at times virtually to the exclusion of all other aspects of the play. But there have also been other approaches, reflected in titles such as the "unity," the "imagery," the "world," or the "meaning" of *Hamlet*.

Such approaches may share one advantage: through them critic and reader alike are easily led to believe that a dramatic pattern has been established into which the controversial hero will necessarily fit—the problems of his character may in other words be solved largely by ignoring them. This is too convenient a short cut to be disregarded in a lecture, and I shall certainly make use of it. The character of the hero will, however, hardly be ignored. My subject is judgment in *Hamlet* the play, where the character judged is Hamlet the man.

It is a commonplace to refer to Hamlet's "dilemma" and a critical problem to explain in what this dilemma consists. A natural way to come to terms with the problem is obviously through the character that forces the dilemma upon Hamlet, that is to say, the Ghost. This is a particularly attractive approach, since it promises to bring the findings of modern research into Elizabethan demonology to bear directly upon the question of the nature of the Ghost and its message. It was apparently generally believed, among Catholics and Protestants alike, that a ghost could be dispatched into this world by either God or the devil, and consequently it became the duty of the receiver of its command to test it conscientiously before acting upon it. This is what we see Hamlet do when, in spite of his immediate conviction that it is an honest ghost he has seen, he arranges a trial of its veracity in the form of the play within the play. The answer that he gets is unmistakable: the King is guilty, the Ghost's story confirmed, and the apparition itself an emissary from heaven.

The main objection to this argument is obvious. The Ghost demands blood-revenge, and it would seem to be out of character for an agent of good to engage in such a mission. The standard answer to this used to be that Shakespeare and his contemporaries looked upon revenge as a legitimate alternative to the punishment meted out by the law, particularly if the offended party could not expect to bring his adversary to justice by due process—essentially Hamlet's situation. But the answer is unsatisfactory. There are indeed Elizabethan writers who argue in this vein, but they are rare and hardly representative, being frequently fencing-masters and almost to a man admirers of the duelling code that had already led to a serious decimation of young bloods in France. Responsible individuals—statesmen, magistrates, and clergymen alike —unanimously condemned such conduct, and I find it impossible to believe that Shakespeare, who presented Brutus' dilemma and the consequences of his choice with such moral and psychological insight, could have accepted the revenger's code of honor.

An equally familiar and somewhat more plausible argument may also be adduced to explain the significance of the Ghost: Shakespeare, like his fellow dramatists, did not personally regard blood-revenge as justified but followed the so-called revenge convention of the Elizabethan theatre. Dramatic heroes were, in other words, traditionally supposed to have the

right to revenge the deaths of their kinsmen, provided that they did not resort to such un-English
methods as poisoning or allow their desire for vengeance to express itself in the form of indiscriminate
murder, in the manner of Titus Andronicus or Old
Hieronymo. The tradition, however, is by no means
so simple. True enough, from 1592 to 1607 we have
what at times looks deceptively like a stage debate on
the question of the justification of revenge, but in no
completed play except Marston's *Antonio's Revenge*,
a product which it is very difficult to take seriously,
would I say that revenge is presented as justified beyond doubt. Somewhere in the execution of his duty
the revenger seems to go wrong and develop into a
creature that must not be allowed to survive. Thus, no
matter how closely Shakespeare considered himself
obliged to follow his sources—which do accept revenge as the order of nature—it is a demonstrable mistake to say that he had to follow a strong dramatic
tradition. First, he did not have to and, second, the
tradition was rather in the opposite direction.

This argument would seem to lead to an unpleasant
conclusion: Hamlet's attempt to test the Ghost's veracity ends in a failure to discover the truth; the
Ghost is actually the devil's emissary, and Hamlet follows the advice of the devil when he plans and finally
executes his revenge. But this, I would say, is only apparently so; the real situation is different. In the
tragedy of *Hamlet* Shakespeare does not concern himself with the question whether blood-revenge is justi-

fied or not; it is raised only once and very late by the protagonist (v,ii,63–70) and never seriously considered. The dramatic and psychological situation rather than the moral issue is what seems to have attracted Shakespeare, and he chose to develop it, in spite of the hard-to-digest and at times a little absurd elements it might involve, as he did in *Twelfth Night,* in *King Lear,* and in *Cymbeline.* What we have in *Hamlet* is thus a situation where the hero sincerely and profoundly feels that he is under an absolute obligation to revenge his father's death. He feels it as his duty, and we, spectators and readers alike, should accept his feelings as genuine, irrespective of our own opinions. The duty lies heavy on him, it is foreign to his nature, but he feels in honor bound to fulfill it—this lies at the heart of Hamlet's dilemma, not the question whether or not revenge is morally justified. If we adhere to this necessary and perhaps not altogether elementary distinction, the play will be easier to understand.

It will first of all become clearer what the grouping of characters against Hamlet implies. Since the nature of the Ghost remains ambiguous and there is no safe association between Hamlet and the devil or between Hamlet and God, we have to rely on the impression that his opponents make on us, on first appearance and in revealing scenes together—a standard procedure, I would say, in the interpretation of any Shakespearean play. Of course we should realize that Claudius is presented as a capable ruler and a resourceful man—as

Shakespeare also drew Richard III—but this should not interfere with our dominant impression of him.

Though yet of Hamlet our dear brother's death
The memory be green; and that it us befitted
To bear our hearts in grief, and our whole kingdom
To be contracted in one brow of woe;
Yet so far hath discretion fought with nature
That we with wisest sorrow think on him,
Together with remembrance of ourselves. . . .

From this first speech of his, with its uncomfortably balanced periods and forced vocabulary, the audience should feel ill at ease in his presence, even though they may find it hard to realize that he is the rankest and grossest of the things in nature which Hamlet condemns. After the revelations of the Ghost there should certainly be little hesitation: Claudius is classified first as "that incestuous, that adulterate beast" and then as a "smiling, damned villain," two verdicts which, for all their emotional bias, are never seriously questioned in the play.

This is not to overlook the King's devotion to his painfully acquired wife or thoughtful attention to his exasperating stepson, nor is it to ignore his pangs of conscience when Polonius unwittingly touches him to the quick:

How smart a lash that speech doth give my conscience!
The harlot's cheek, beautied with plast'ring art,
Is not more ugly to the thing that helps it

Than is my deed to my most painted word.
O, heavy burden!

It is above all not to neglect his desperate and moving but, as he himself knows, futile prayer to be forgiven for the murder of his brother. A villain is, after all, still a human being, and Claudius' attempts to repent stress the humanity of the man without deleting the villainy which, very soon, reasserts itself in the plots against Hamlet's life.

Of the minor weeds which disturb Hamlet, Polonius is the most troublesome. We know that his advice to Ophelia and Laertes closely parallels the wisdom that eminently respectable Elizabethan fathers bestowed on their children; prudence was a more commendable virtue in the Renaissance than now, and the sentiment of "This above all, to thine own self be true" remains, I should hope, unexceptionable today. But Polonius' prudence, loyalty to the King, and pitiful death in his service do not make him the "good old man" that the Queen sees in him. He is a gentleman of the situation who, for his own and his master's purposes, manipulates human beings, including his own children, and who does not even do it very well. Like Claudius he is a plausible individual, not a monster, but unlike Claudius he appears to have grown morally blind—a verdict which, in due course, would evidently have applied also to the more immature manipulators Rosencrantz and Guildenstern, whose loyalty to the King seems to know no reservations. With Queen

Gertrude and finally also Laertes deeply involved in a situation of increasing ugliness, it becomes clear that, although Claudius and those who associate with him are not the incarnations of evil that Hamlet sees in them, they are corrupt enough from any balanced point of view, a condition that is also intimated by the "heavy-headed revel" that distinguishes life at the Danish court. The only character who is presented almost entirely as a victim is Ophelia, a victim of the King's fear and curiosity, her father's servility and fundamental indifference to her, Hamlet's misunderstanding of the situation and brutal treatment of her, and finally his fatal thrust through the arras in the closet scene. Her madness is, as I see it, a purely pathetic element in the play. In the world where Hamlet has been forced to act, there appears to be no room for passive and obedient innocence. It is crushed, and perishes.

It is of course a euphemism to say that Ophelia "perishes." Hamlet is indirectly responsible for her death, as he is directly for her father's, Rosencrantz', and Guildenstern's. It is indeed easy to understand why critics have called Hamlet an agent of death, particularly if we remember with what peculiar indifference he expresses himself on the fate of his victims. His farewell to Polonius is familiar:

Thou wretched, rash, intruding fool, farewell!
I took thee for thy better. Take thy fortune;
Thou find'st to be too busy is some danger.

And his comment on the execution of his former friends has the same unconcerned ring:

Why, man, they did make love to this employment;
They are not near my conscience; their defeat
Does by their own insinuation grow.

It is thus clear that if, either instinctively or deliberately, we find it impossible to regard Hamlet as an agent of death in any but the most literal sense of the words, we must produce some explanation of this callousness, in Hamlet's situation and in our concept of his character. We must be prepared for an analysis of the part which has been the object of more analyses than I care to remember. Like all such analyses it will be arbitrary; since I have chosen to concentrate on Hamlet's development rather than on his static qualities, I shall for instance have no observations to make on the wit which is indeed an essential quality of the character.

Let us then first clarify Hamlet's initial situation, as it is presented to us in the first great soliloquy "O, that this too too solid flesh would melt." It is a statement that is unusually easy to understand. The death of his father has shaken Hamlet so profoundly that he refuses to accept it as natural, and he takes the same attitude to the remarriage of his mother, which to us would seem to belong to a different category. If this is what goes on in the world—for to Hamlet and other young idealists their world is the world—the emotional state of misanthropy obviously offers an escape, particularly since the logical escape of suicide is not open to him. Hamlet's pessimism is thus an already existing state of mind, a burden which the Ghost makes still heavier for him to bear. For while the supernatural message gives Hamlet a strong incitement to act, it also reveals to him that the world is even worse than he believed: Claudius has used murder to gain himself a kingdom and a wife. The same Ghost who exhorts Hamlet to revenge feeds his misanthropy. The natural order demands action from him, when he has already begun to doubt the validity of that order.

The sequence of thought that follows upon the appearance of the Ghost is more difficult to interpret. Although for some time Hamlet does not waver in his opinion of its honesty, he is in no state of mind to inflict a successful revenge upon Claudius. He puts on an antic disposition, not in order to find out the truth, since he is convinced that he knows it, nor in order to test Claudius, which he does not even begin to do, but rather, I would say, to be allowed to withdraw within himself and find answers to two complex questions with which he becomes increasingly preoccupied. The first is an expansion of the misanthropic thoughts that plagued him before he knew of the King's guilt: what is the nature of the world in which such monstrosities as he has seen and heard of are allowed to happen? The second is an immediate consequence of the Ghost's demand: what kind of man is he, Hamlet, who somehow feels repelled by the natural duty he is to perform, somehow feels that it is unnatural?

Hamlet's inquiry into the nature of the world is conducted in an experimental fashion. Since Claudius and Gertrude have already been examined to his satisfaction, it now becomes the turn of Polonius, Rosencrantz, and Guildenstern. The experiments are conversational, and since no extenuating circumstances are admitted, they confirm his suspicions that these gentlemen are all lackeys of the King and consequently vile—which makes their professed friendship for him nothing but hypocrisy. With even better reason than before, he feels able to generalize: the earth is a sterile promontory, the air a foul and pestilent congregation of vapors, and man a quintessence of dust. It is an interpretation that will lead to resignation rather than to decisive action, an interpretation that is quite properly further spelled out in the bitter description of life that we know from "To be, or not to be"—life with its

> whips and scorns of time,
> Th' oppressor's wrong, the proud man's contumely,
> The pangs of despis'd love, the law's delay,
> The insolence of office, and the spurns
> That patient merit of th' unworthy takes.

Whether or not these generalizations are true, they are obviously based on an inadequate study of the world. For Hamlet's experiments are emotionally biased and pitifully limited: the presumably crucial question of Ophelia's integrity is never seriously raised, but her lack of it is taken for granted. Hamlet's mind is too easily made up and his conviction accordingly unyielding: the nature of the world, the nature of man, is evil. It is a conviction that is expressed most emphatically in the nunnery scene, where the cessation of human life, at least for the sake of the argument, is considered desirable: "Get thee to a nunnery. Why wouldst thou be a breeder of sinners? I am myself indifferent honest, but yet I could accuse me of such things that it were better my mother had not borne me: I am very proud, revengeful, ambitious; with more offences at my beck than I have thoughts to put them in, imagination to give them shape, or time to act them in. What should such fellows as I do crawling between earth and heaven? We are arrant knaves, all. . . ." And again: "I say, we will have no moe marriage: those that are married already, all but one, shall live; the rest shall keep as they are. To a nunnery, go."

With his treatment of Ophelia in this and the subsequent scene, Hamlet has been said to reach the bottom of his misanthropy; his alienation from the rest of the world seems complete. Yet we notice something that points to a possible way out of this predicament: he uses himself as an example of the corruption of man. This would seem to be a result of the self-examination that begins with "O, what a rogue and peasant slave am I" and ends with "To be, or not to be." The first and highly emotional stage of the inquiry leads to a conclusion that is truly humiliating. The actor who describes Hecuba's grief so vividly that his color changes and his eyes water brings Hamlet's insufficiency as a revenger and a man of action home to him so effectively that he bursts out into unbalanced self-accusations:

> 'Swounds, I should take it; for it cannot be
> But I am pigeon-liver'd and lack gall
> To make oppression bitter, or ere this
> I should 'a fatted all the region kites
> With this slave's offal.

This analysis of himself as a coward is, however, one to which Hamlet no more returns, at least not in despair at his own insufficiency. When, in "To be, or not to be," the subject of his aversion to act against Claudius is again broached, it is considered in a different light. Hamlet's mood has changed: he is no longer desperate, but collected and resigned. The fact of his insufficiency is accepted, and reasons are advanced that explain such shortcomings as general in human life:

> And makes *us* rather bear those ills *we* have
> Than fly to others that *we* know not of?
> Thus conscience does make cowards of *us all*;
> And thus the native hue of resolution
> Is sicklied o'er with the pale cast of thought.[1]

Although the question of why he, Hamlet, cannot perform the specific act of killing his uncle will continue to disturb him, he seems now to have arrived at

---

[1] For the italics, see Theodore Spencer, *Shakespeare and the Nature of Man* (New York, 1961), p. 107.

some understanding of his situation: it is a natural one, which is shared by other men. His alienation from mankind may soon be over.

But the plan proceeds which Hamlet, almost independent of his own speculations, has set in motion in order to lay at rest his doubts about the Ghost's origin and the King's guilt. The peculiar thing about the "mouse-trap" is surely that it is not arranged so as to catch or even to shock Claudius; instead it gives him several opportunities to recognize the situation and adapt himself to it: first the dumb-show with its not particularly obscure acting-out of the plot, then the Player Queen's lines "In second husband let me be accurst! None wed the second but who kill'd the first," and finally the elaborate preparation for the poisoning, all accompanied by Hamlet's comments, which are nothing if not provocative. It is easy to see that, from a practical point of view, the experiment is a failure, since Claudius departs warned and ready to protect himself. Hamlet, however, has experienced an intellectual and emotional triumph which, to judge from the diffidence of his preparations, is more than he expected, and which will now determine the course that he will follow to the exclusion of the sadder but wiser thoughts of "To be, or not to be."

It is not a pleasant course. After the play we find Hamlet in a peculiar mood. The success which he is enjoying, the certainty which he has gained, the knowledge that there is now no turning back, and the danger which this brings with it—all seems to have created in him a state of mind which is perhaps best characterized as desperate exaltation. He indulges in wild jokes with Horatio; mocks Polonius, Rosencrantz, and Guildenstern more brazenly than ever; and finds himself giving utterance to such bloody thoughts that he has to pull himself up short:

'Tis now the very witching time of night,
When churchyards yawn and hell itself breathes out
Contagion to this world. Now could I drink hot blood,
And do such bitter business as the day
Would quake to look on.

It is in this irresponsible mood that he discovers Claudius at his prayers and abstains from killing him, because it would be "hire and salary, not revenge" to "take him in the purging of his soul,/When he is fit and season'd for his passage," instead of waiting until "his soul may be as damn'd and black/As hell, whereto it goes." The speech has been condemned as utterly cruel and foreign to Hamlet. Cruel it is, but foreign to the Hamlet we know it is not. Once he certainly was "noble Hamlet," and vestiges of this nobility of soul are still to be seen in his moments of reflection and self-questioning. By fits and starts, however, he has been reduced to a haunted and desperate young man, who is now, I would say, almost hysterically riding the wave of his exaltation.

It is on his way to his mother that Hamlet overhears the King's prayer, and he is in the same dangerous mood when he confronts her in order, as he says, to "speak daggers to her, but use none." Actually he speaks sledgehammers rather than daggers:

> O shame! where is they blush?
> Rebellious hell,
> If thou canst mutine in a matron's bones,
> To flaming youth let virtue be as wax
> And melt in her own fire; proclaim no shame
> When the compulsive ardour gives the charge,
> Since frost itself as actively doth burn,
> And reason panders will.

His words are obviously intended to shock the Queen into a recognition of what her union with Claudius means, at least to her son, but Hamlet's misanthropy, always rooted in his mother's behavior, takes control of his thoughts. Here, as frequently in his speeches, sexuality is made to stand for evil, a natural process for the nature of man. The violence of his outbursts is extreme: at times he seems to rave without being able to check himself. The exaltation stays with him long after he has killed Polonius.

Hamlet's immediate reaction to this deed is indifference or, even worse, satisfaction:

> Heaven hath pleas'd it so,
> To punish me with this, and this with me,
> That I must be their scourge and minister.

This smug attitude, however, is not maintained for long: indifference and self-satisfaction are mixed with despair in the speeches to the King, Rosencrantz, and

Guildenstern that follow the closet-scene. The antic disposition is undoubtedly present, but imperfectly hidden under it is a genuine wildness, to which the chain of events that began with the performance of the "mouse trap" has now led. For it is a horrible and unreasonable crime of which Hamlet has made himself guilty, a crime that implies that all his earnest attempts to reconcile the voice of nature with the voice of his nature have utterly failed: he has become a murderer, not a revenger—hence his despair. But Polonius' death has also showed him the way to achieve his duty— hence his self-satisfaction. His only possibility lies in ceasing to think "too precisely on th' event"; the excitements of his reason and his blood must be allowed to spur him on, until a stage has been reached where his thoughts will be "bloody, or be nothing worth." Since the nature of man is evil, why not accept the consequence in earnest—that his, Hamlet's, nature is also evil—and act accordingly: take revenge no matter in what manner, no matter what the cost, no matter what his feelings. Having reached this practical simplification of the problem, Hamlet departs for England. In harmony with it he sends Rosencrantz and Guildenstern to their death.

We soon discover, however, that when Hamlet returns his thoughts are no longer bloody. He asks Horatio once whether it would not be "perfect conscience" to kill the King, but he does not press the point. His thoughts, which now move in a quietly meditative fashion, center on the phenomenon of death and what he suspects is his own impending death. The idea of mortality has fascinated him before, but in the grave-digger scene his argument does not take him further into misanthropy, but instead to a sardonic acceptance of inevitable facts: "Alexander died, Alexander was buried, Alexander returneth to dust; the dust is earth; of earth we make loam, and why of that loam whereto he was converted might they not stop a beer-barrel?" Another aspect of his dearly bought balance of mind is evident in his conversations with Horatio, while the preparations are being made for the fencing match. Here his indifference to the future seems complete: heaven saved him from death on the way to England; let heaven now see to it that Hamlet serves its purposes during the short time he has left. This makes it possible for him to accept Laertes' challenge, even though, as he admits to Horatio, "thou wouldst not think how ill all 's here about my heart." His submission to what he calls "heaven" and "a divinity that shapes our ends" is in fact so pronounced that it is tempting to interpret the special providence that he sees in the fall of a sparrow in a very Christian manner: Hamlet seems to have left his vengeance in the hands of the Lord.

Without claiming much knowledge of what submission to God should mean, I must, however, point out the basic weakness of this interpretation. One should, as far as I can see, submit to God's will with joy, satisfaction, or at least a positive conviction, and there is no sign of this in the case of Hamlet. When he

allows things to happen to him, he does it in the belief
that everything which takes place will be for the best
and that he is no longer capable of performing his mission of revenge. The acceptance of the purposes of a
Power above him implies a personal defeat, which
cannot but rankle within him. He has arrived at a new
answer to the question of his own nature, an answer
quite different from the cruel alternative in "How all
occasions do inform against me," but equally simpli-
fied: since he seems to be constitutionally unable to
extract revenge from Claudius, the revenge itself
should be abandoned. Why he labors under this inability is a question that he tries no longer to be concerned with. His attempts to do his duty have cost too
much—not only Polonius' but also Ophelia's life. All
that now remains is to act out the final scene in as dig-
nified a manner as possible.

This is also what we see Hamlet do. His behavior to
Laertes before and during the fencing match is sincere
and chivalrous, so noble indeed that his opponent feels
that it is almost against his conscience to kill him.
Almost, but not quite. Hamlet is wounded to death,
the truth is revealed, and the King immediately
stabbed—whereupon Hamlet forces the poisoned
drink down his victim's throat, with words that recall
earlier situations, the Ghost's message, and Hamlet's
mission:

Here, thou incestuous, murd'rous, damned Dane.
Drink off this potion. Is thy union here?
Follow my mother.

Another cruel and shocking deed? Yes, beyond doubt. Let us, however, consider what happens a little more precisely. Why does Hamlet, in his last moments, when the King is presumably mortally wounded, thus add horror to horror? The reason may not be pleasant, but it is deeply rooted in man's nature: Hamlet finally sees an opportunity to do what the Ghost had told him, do it deliberately, ritually, and publicly, and he seizes it in order to satisfy at least himself. Right and wrong no longer matter; self-esteem is more important. He is able to vindicate his integrity in his own eyes. Whereupon he asks Horatio to do him the same service in the eyes of the world—and dies:

Now cracks a noble heart. Good night, sweet prince,
And flights of angels sing thee to thy rest!

Are we supposed to join in this expression of hope? What is the judgment passed on Hamlet the man in Shakespeare's tragedy? Our impressions of Hamlet as he was before his father's death must necessarily be fragmentary and personal; according to Ophelia he was "th' expectancy and rose of the fair state," with a mind that was above all "noble." To us, however, this "noble Hamlet" will have to remain a possibility, an ideal; to many, an illusion. What we have seen is how a hypersensitive, hyperintelligent, and witty, but sadly inexperienced and morally unsophisticated young man is shaken to the core of his being by intimate contact with what he considers unprecedented evil. We have seen how, in this vulnerable state of discovery and disillusion, he is commanded, by the order of nature that he has begun to question, to perform a duty from which his own nature recoils. To solve this dilemma to both his own and the Ghost's satisfaction is impossible—a fact, however, which Hamlet will not realize. His course thus becomes one from one state of despair to another. We have seen how the despair of thought, which at least makes him begin to understand the nature of his dilemma, gives way to the despair of action, which promises success but makes him a murderer. We have seen how he then recedes into the despair of resignation, the negative balance of mind which the sorely tried may achieve by accepting the horrors of life as inevitable and natural. Hamlet's education in the ways of the world is over, and the discrepancy between expectation and fact, intention and execution, ideal and reality, has become too much for him to bear in any other way. We have finally seen how Hamlet, to whom this development has been a personal defeat, sees a last possibility to change defeat into a token victory, takes it, and asserts himself and his *virtù*—no more, but also no less—to himself and to the world, after Shakespeare has called forth the vision of "noble Hamlet" for the last time.

The problem of Hamlet may thus largely be one of attitude. If we can learn to look upon the hero neither as an ideal figure nor as an agent of death, but as a young man both bewildered and analytical, at the mercy of circumstances rather than in command of them, in the power of his emotions rather than of his thoughts, with a strong sense of self-respect as well as of moral values, then we shall come closer to him and to a realization of the intrinsic unity of the play. This will not make its ultimate effect simple—far from it. The feeling of waste, that something precious and irreplaceable has been lost when Hamlet dies, is strong and essential. The feeling of relief, that death comes as a liberator to Hamlet, is equally strong and equally essential. The feeling of victory, that, to his own satisfaction, Hamlet has triumphed over himself, is problematic and will always make the impact of the ending complex and disturbing. Further I do not believe that Shakespeare goes, and further we need not go. If we wish, we may, however, view Hamlet's dilemma from yet another perspective: he cannot exact vengeance, since he vaguely feels that the Ghost, in spite of proof to the contrary, is an emissary of the devil; the end of the play would then show us how Hamlet, against all reason, falls victim to an inhuman code of duty when he kills Claudius. By not commenting on it Shakespeare has made the perspective possible. Whether we reject or accept it, we should have charity and self-knowledge enough to let flights of angels sing Hamlet to his rest.

"We Came Crying Hither":

An Essay on Some Characteristics of
King Lear

BY MAYNARD MACK

I HAVE chosen *King Lear* for my topic in this essay, written in honor of Shakespeare's quatercentenary, in the belief that it is peculiarly the play of his that speaks with urgency to our time. The other tragedies to a far larger extent, it seems to me, abide our question; *King Lear* is free. It stands there like Hopkins' mind mountain—

> cliffs of fall,
> Frightful, sheer, no-man-fathomed—

its abysses wrapped in the enigma of our own ignorance of the meaning of existence, its peaks echoing with cries of triumph and despair that we are hardly sure are not ours.

Partly the play teases us because we have only lately recaptured it as a play. We have no records of its effectiveness in performance before the closing of the theatres in 1642 nor during the interval between their reopening and 1681. But from that year until 1838, Shakespeare's *King Lear* was seen on the stage only in the revision by Nahum Tate, who gave it a happy ending and made other changes too silly to mention here. Tate's happy ending, in which Cordelia is spared to marry Edgar and King Lear retrieves his kingdom, may be looked on as the appropriate expression of an age deeply convinced that there was an order of justice underlying the appearances of things which it was the function of literature to reveal and imitate, not to hide.

A hundred and fifty-seven years later, Macready rescued the play from its neoclassic trappings, but he and his successors continued to hold it at arm's length. They historicized it, situated it among Druids, or in ancient Britain immediately after the departure of the Romans, swathed all its fierce edges in scene-changes, realistic storm effects, and trees with individual leaves that shook. This way of dealing with the play was the natural expression of an age whose best poet (who happily did not often practice his preachment) said that poetry was made of the real language of real men, and whose most systematic critic believed he had engaged what was important about literature when he talked of "race," "milieu," "moment." It is only today that audiences may again hope to see this play performed in something approaching its original grandeur, as a work of the mythic imagination to which a comparable imaginative response must be made if we are not to be put off by its stiff allegorisms, on the one hand, its melodramatic implausibilities, on the other.

It may be that the play also draws us because its "tragic-heroic" content, like that of our contemporary plays, is ambiguous and impure. This is not simply to refer to its well-known vein of grotesqueries, or those events and speeches which have the character of poignant farce and even of inspired music-hall fooling, like the Fool's mouthings, Edgar's gyrations, Gloucester's leap. The play does blur the ordinary tragic-heroic norms. Consider the death of the protagonist, for instance. This is usually in Shakespeare climactic and distinctive, has sacrificial implications, dresses itself in ritual, springs from what we know to be a Renaissance mystique of stoical self-dominion. How differently death comes to Lear! Not in a moment of self-scrutiny that stirs us to awe or exaltation or regret at waste, but as a blessing at which we must rejoice with Kent, hardly more than a needful afterthought to the death that counts dramatically, Cordelia's. To die with no salute to death, with the whole consciousness launched toward another; to die following a life-experience in which what we have been shown to admire is far more the capacity to endure than to perform: this is unique in Shakespeare, and sits more easily with our present sensibility (which is pathologically mistrustful of heroism) than the heroic resonances of the usual Shakespearean close.

The miscellaneousness and very casualness of death

in *King Lear* is perhaps also something to which the generations that know Auschwitz are attuned. In the other tragedies, as a student of mine has noticed in an interesting unpublished paper, there is always a hovering suggestion that death is noble, that the great or good, having done the deed or followed the destiny that was in them to do or follow, go out in a blaze of light. So Romeo and Juliet seem to go. So Cleopatra goes, turning to air and fire to meet Mark Antony. Hamlet goes in a glimpse of some felicity, Othello in a recollection of a deed of derring-do and justice, even Macbeth in a kind of negative glory like the transcendent criminal he has become. But *King Lear* repudiates this: "The dramatic emphasis is on the generality of death; death is not noble or distinctive; nearly every character dies and for nearly every sort of reason. The reiterated fact of the multiple deaths is processional in quality. It is like an enormous summarial obituary. The Fool disappears of causes mysterious; Oswald, tailormade servant, is killed by Edgar; Goneril and Regan are poisoned and dagger-slain; Gloucester dies offstage of weariness, conflicting emotion, and a broken heart; Kent is about to die of grief and service; Edmund is killed by his brother in a duel; Cordelia dies (by a kind of mistake—'Great thing of us forgot!') at a hangman's hands; and King Lear dies of grief and deluded joy and fierce exhaustion. . . . Death is neither punishment nor reward: it is simply in the nature of things."

To this we may add, I think, a third factor that

brings *King Lear* close to our business and bosoms today. Intimations of World's End run through it like a yeast. In the scenes on the heath, the elements are at war as if it were indeed Armageddon. When Lear awakes with Cordelia at his side, he imagines that already Apocalypse is past, she is a soul in bliss, he bound upon a wheel of fire. Appearing in the last act with Cordelia dead in his arms, he wonders that those around him do not crack "heaven's vault" with their grief, and they wonder in turn if the *pietà* they behold is "the promis'd end" or "image of that horror." These are but some of the overt allusions. Under them everywhere run tides of doomsday passion that seem to use up and wear away people, codes, expectations, all stable points of reference, till only a profound sense remains that an epoch, in fact a whole dispensation, has forever closed.

> The oldest hath borne most: we that are young
> Shall never see so much, nor live so long.

To this kind of situation, we of the mid-twentieth century are likewise sensitively attuned. I shall quote from another student, partly because the comment is eloquent, but chiefly because I think it is significant that everywhere in the 1950's and 1960's the young are responding to *King Lear* as never before in my experience. "Every great critic," this student writes, "from Johnson on, including many who were and are hostile to the play, at some time or other begins to think of the sea. The most moving example of this common image, perhaps, is Hazlitt's: he speaks of the passion of King Lear as resembling an ocean, 'swelling, chafing, raging, without bound, without hope, without beacon, or anchor,' and of how on the sea Lear 'floats, a mighty wreck in the wide world of sorrows.' . . . The sea plays no direct part in the action. But the smell of it and the sound of it are omnipresent. The sea licks up at Dover relentlessly, its 'murmuring surge' is endless and inescapable and everywhere—an archetype not of an individual drowning, but of the flooding of the world. *King Lear* is alive again: it is our myth, our dream, as we stand naked and unaccommodated, listening to the water rise up against our foothold on the cliff of chalk."

This statement is incomplete. It leaves out of account the strong undertow of victory in the play which carves on those same chalk walls Lear's "new acquist" of self-knowledge and devotion to Cordelia, the majesty of his integrity and endurance, the invincibleness of his hope. These give to an audience's applauses at the close of a great performance a quality of exaltation. The statement is incomplete; but what it includes and what it leaves out both make clear why *King Lear* above all others is the Shakespearean tragedy for our time.

i i

I turn now to the play. In the pages that follow, I wish to make primarily three comments: one on the special character of its action, one on the special character of the world in which this action is housed, and one, stemming from both of these, on what I take to be the play's tragic theme, summed up best in Lear's words to Gloucester in Dover fields: "We came crying hither."

As we watch it in the theatre, *King Lear* comes to us first of all as an experience of violence and pain. No other Shakespearean tragedy, not even *Titus*, contains more levels of raw ferocity, physical as well as moral. In the action, the exquisite cruelties of Goneril and Regan to their father are capped by Gloucester's blinding onstage, and this in turn by the wanton indignity of Cordelia's murder. In the language, as Miss Spurgeon has pointed out, allusions to violence multiply and accumulate into a pervasive image as of "a human body in anguished movement—tugged, wrenched, beaten, pierced, stung, dislocated, flayed, scalded, tortured, and finally broken on the rack."

Miss Spurgeon's comment formulates the play in terms of passiveness and suffering. But the whole truth is not seen unless it is formulated also in terms of agency and aggression. If the Lear world is exceptionally anguished, it is partly because it is exceptionally contentious. Tempers in *King Lear* heat so fast that some critics are content to see in it simply a tragedy of wrath. Unquestionably it does contain a remarkable number of remarkably passionate collisions. Lear facing Cordelia, and Kent facing Lear, in the opening scene; Lear confronting Goneril at her house with his terrifying curse; Kent tangling with

Oswald outside Gloucester's castle; Cornwall run through by his own servant, who warns Regan that if she had a beard he'd "shake it on this quarrel"; Edgar and Edmund simulating a scuffle in the first act, and later, in the last act, hurling charge and counter-charge in the scene of their duel; the old King himself defying the storm: these are only the more vivid instances of a pattern of pugnacity which pervades this tragedy from beginning to end, shrilling the voices that come to us from the stage and coloring their language even in the tenderest scenes. The pattern gives rise to at least one locution which in frequency of occurrence is peculiar to *King Lear*—to "outface the winds and persecutions of the sky," to "outscorn the to-and-fro contending wind and rain," to "outjest his heart-struck injuries," to "outfrown false Fortune's frown." And it appears as a motif even in that pitful scene at Dover, where the old King, at first alone, throws down his glove before an imaginary opponent—"There's my gauntlet, I'll prove it on a giant"—and, afterward, when the blind Gloucester enters, defies him too: "No, do thy worst, blind Cupid, I'll not love." So powerful is this vein of belligerence in the linguistic texture of the play that pity itself is made, in Cordelia's words, something that her father's white hairs must "challenge." Even "had you not been their father," she says, in an apostrophe to the sleeping King, referring to the suffering he has been caused by his other daughters, "these white flakes/Did challenge pity of them."

It goes without saying that in a world of such contentiousness most of the *dramatis personae* will be out-
rageously self-assured. The contrast with the situation
in *Hamlet*, in this respect, is striking and instructive.
There, as I have argued in another place, the prevail-
ing mood tends to be interrogative. Doubt is real in
Hamlet, and omnipresent. Minds, even villainous
minds, are inquiet and uncertain. Action does not
come readily to anyone except Laertes and Fortinbras,
who are themselves easily deflected by the stratagems
of the King, and there is accordingly much emphasis
on the fragility of the human will. All this is changed
in *King Lear*. Its mood, I would suggest (if it may be
caught in a single word at all), is imperative. The
play asks questions, to be sure, as *Hamlet* does, and far
more painful questions because they are so like a
child's, so simple and unmediated by the compromises
to which much experience usually impels us: "Is man
no more than this?" "Is there any cause in nature that
makes these hard hearts?"—"Why should a dog, a
horse, a rat have life/And thou no breath at all?"
Such questionings in *King Lear* stick deep, like Macbeth's fears in Banquo.

Yet it is not, I think, the play's questions that establish its distinctive coloring onstage. It is rather its commands, its invocations and appeals that have the quality of commands, its flat-footed defiances and refusals:
"Come not between the dragon and his wrath"—
"You nimble lightnings, dart your blinding flames
into her scornful eyes"—"Blow, winds, crack your

cheeks! rage! blow!—"Thou shalt not die; die for adul-
tery, no!"—"A plague upon you murderers, traitors,
all! I might have saved her." In the psychological cli-
mate that forms round a protagonist like this, there is
little room for doubt, as we may see from both Lear's
and Goneril's scorn of Albany. No villain's mind is
unquiet. Action comes as naturally as breathing and
twice as quick. And, what is particularly unlike the
situation in the earlier tragedies, the hero's destiny is
self-made. Lear does not inherit this predicament like
Hamlet; he is not duped by an antagonist like
Othello. He walks into disaster head-on.

   This difference is of the first importance. *King Lear*,
to follow R. W. Chambers in applying Keats's memorable phrase, is a vale of soul-making, where the will
is agonizingly free. As if to force the point on our attention, almost every character in the play, including
such humble figures as Cornwall's servant and the old
tenant who befriends Gloucester, is impelled soon or
late to take some sort of stand—to show, in Oswald's
words, "what party I do follow." One cannot but be
struck by how much positioning and repositioning of
this kind the play contains. Lear at first takes up his
position with Goneril and Regan, France and Kent
take theirs with Cordelia, Albany takes his with
Goneril, and Gloucester with Cornwall and Regan.
But then all reposition. Kent elects to come back as
his master's humblest servant. The Fool elects to stay
with the great wheel, even though it runs downhill.
Lear elects to become a comrade of the wolf and owl

rather than return to his elder daughters. Gloucester likewise has second thoughts and comes to Lear's rescue, gaining his sight though he loses his eyes. Albany has second thoughts and lives, he says, only to revenge those eyes. In the actions of the old King himself, the taking of yet a third position is possibly implied. For after the battle, when Cordelia asks, "Shall we not see these daughters and these sisters?" Lear replies (with the vehemence characteristic of him even in defeat), "No, no, no, no!" and goes on to build, in his famous following lines, that world entirely free of pugnacity and contentiousness in which he and Cordelia will dwell: "We two alone will sing like birds i' th' cage."

Movements of the will, then, have a featured place in *King Lear*. But what is more characteristic of the play than their number is the fact that no one of them is ever exhibited to us in its inward origins or evolution. Instead of scenes according to the genesis or gestation of an action—scenes of introspection or persuasion or temptation like those which occupy the heart of the drama in *Hamlet*, *Othello*, and *Macbeth* —*King Lear* offers us the moment at which will converts into its outward expressions of action and consequence, and this fact, I suspect, helps account for the special kind of painfulness that the play always communicates to its audiences. In *King Lear* we are not permitted to experience violence as an externalization of a psychological drama which has priority in both time and significance, and which therefore partly palliates the violence when it comes. This is how we do experience, I think, Hamlet's vindictiveness to his mother, Macbeth's massacres, Othello's murder: the act in the outer world is relieved of at least part of its savagery by our understanding of the inner act behind it. The violences in *King Lear* are thrust upon us quite otherwise—with the shock that comes from evil which has nowhere been inwardly accounted for, and which, from what looks like a studiedly uninward point of view on the playwright's part, must remain unaccountable, to characters and audience alike: "Is there any cause in nature that makes these hard hearts?"

iii

The relatively slight attention given in *King Lear* to the psychological processes that ordinarily precede and determine human action suggests that here we may be meant to look for meaning in a somewhat different quarter from that in which we find it in the earlier tragedies. In *Hamlet*, Shakespeare had explored action in its aspect of dilemma. Whether or not we accept the traditional notion that Hamlet is a man who cannot make up his mind, his problem is clearly conditioned by the unsatisfactory nature of the alternatives he faces. Any action involves him in a kind of guilt, the more so because he feels an already existing corruption in himself and in his surroundings which contaminates all action at source. "Virtue cannot so inoculate our old stock but we shall relish of it."

Hence the focus of the play is on those processes of
consciousness which can explain and justify suspension of the will. In *Othello*, by contrast, Shakespeare
seems to be exploring action in its aspect of error.
Othello faces two ways of understanding love—
which is almost to say, in the play's terms, two systems of valuing and two ways of being—but we are
left in no doubt that one of the ways is wrong. Even
if we take Iago and Desdemona, as some critics do,
to be dramatic emblems of conflicting aspects in
Othello's own nature, the play remains a tragedy of
error, not a tragedy of dilemma. "The pity of it,
Iago" is that Othello makes the wrong choice when
the right one is open to him and keeps clamoring to be
known for what it is even to the very moment of the
murder. The playwright's focus in this play is therefore on the corruptions of mind by which a man may
be led into error, and he surrounds Iago and Desdemona with such overtones of damnation and salvation
as ultimately must attend any genuine option between
evil and good.

King Lear, as I see it, confronts the perplexity and
mystery of human action at a later point. Choice remains in the forefront of the argument, but its psychic
antecedents have been so effectively shrunk down in
this primitivized world that action seems to spring directly out of the bedrock of personality. We feel sure
no imaginable psychological process could make Kent
other than loyal, Goneril other than cruel, Edgar
other than "a brother noble." The meaning of action,

here, appears to lie rather in its effects than in antecedents, and particularly in its capacity, as with Lear's in the opening scene, to generate energies that will hurl themselves in unforeseen and unforeseeable reverberations of disorder from end to end of the world.

The elements of that opening scene are worth pausing over, because they seem to have been selected to bring before us precisely such an impression of unpredictable effects lying coiled and waiting in an apparently innocuous posture of affairs. The atmosphere of the first episode in the scene, as many a commentator has remarked, is casual, urbane, even relaxed. In the amenities exchanged by Kent and Gloucester, Shakespeare allows no hint to penetrate of Gloucester's later agitation about "these late eclipses," or about the folly of a king's abdicating his responsibilities and dividing up his power. We are momentarily lulled into a security that is not immediately broken even when the court assembles and Lear informs us that he will shake off all business and "unburthened crawl toward death." I suspect we are invited to sense, as Lear speaks, that this is a kingdom too deeply swaddled in forms of all kinds—too comfortable and secure in its "robes and furred gowns"; in its rituals of authority and deference (of which we have just heard and witnessed samples as Gloucester is dispatched offstage, the map demanded, and a "fast intent" and "constant will" thrust on our notice by the King's imperious personality); and in its childish charades, like the one about to be enacted when the daughters speak. Possibly we are invited to sense, too, that this is in some sort an emblematic kingdom—almost a paradigm of hierarchy and rule, as indeed the scene before us seems to be suggesting, with its wide display of ranks in both family and state. Yet perhaps too schematized, too regular—a place where complex realities have been too much reduced to formulas, as they are on a map: as they are on that visible map, for instance, on which Lear three times lays his finger in this scene ("as if he were marking the land itself," says Granville-Barker), while he describes with an obvious pride its tidy catalogue of "shadowy forests" and "champaigns," "plenteous rivers and wide-skirted meads." Can it be that here, as on that map, is a realm where everything is presumed to have been charted, where all the boundaries are believed known, including those of nature and human nature; but where no account has been taken of the heath which lies in all countries and in all men and women just *beyond* the boundaries they think they know?

However this may be, into this emblematic, almost dreamlike, situation erupts the mysterious thrust of psychic energy that we call a choice, an act; and the waiting coil of consequences leaps into threatening life, bringing with it, as every act considered absolutely must, the inscrutable where we had supposed all was clear, the unexpected though we thought we had envisaged all contingencies and could never be surprised. Perhaps it is to help us see this that the consequences in the play are made so spectacular. The first consequence is Lear's totally unlooked for redistribution of his kingdom into two parts instead of three, and his rejection of Cordelia. The second is his totally unlooked for banishment of his most trusted friend and counselor. The third is the equally unlooked for rescue of his now beggared child to be the Queen of France; and what the unlooked for fourth and fifth will be, we already guess from the agreement between Goneril and Regan, as the scene ends, that something must be done, "and i' th' heat." Thereafter the play seems to illustrate, with an almost diagrammatic relentlessness and thoroughness, the unforeseen potentials that lie waiting to be hatched from a single choice and act: nakedness issues out of opulence, madness out of sanity and reason out of madness, blindness out of seeing and insight out of blindness, salvation out of ruin. The pattern of the unexpected is so completely worked out, in fact, that it appears to embrace even such minor devices of the plot as the fact that Edmund, his fortune made by two letters, is undone by a third.

Meantime, as we look back over the first scene, we may wonder whether the gist of the whole matter has not been placed before us, in the play's own emblematic terms, by Gloucester, Kent, and Edmund in that brief conversation with which the tragedy begins. This conversation touches on two actions, we now observe, each loaded with menacing possibilities, but treated with a casualness at this point that resembles Lear's in opening his trial of love. The first action alluded to is the old King's action in dividing his kingdom, the dire effects of which we are almost instantly

to see. The other action is Gloucester's action in be-
getting a bastard son, and the dire effects of this will
also speedily be known. What is particularly striking,
however, is that in the latter instance the principal
effect is already on the stage before us, though its nature is undisclosed, in the person of the bastard son
himself. Edmund, like other "consequences" looks
tolerable enough till revealed in full: "I cannot wish
the fault undone, the issue of it being so proper," says
Kent, meaning by proper "handsome"; yet there is a
further dimension of meaning in the word that he and
we will only later understand. Like other consequences, too, Edmund looks to be predictable and
manageable—in advance. "He hath been out nine
years," says Gloucester, who has never had any trouble holding consequences at arm's length before, "and
away he shall again." Had Shakespeare reflected on
the problem consciously—and it would be rash, I
think, to be too sure he did not—he could hardly
have chosen a more vivid way of giving dramatic substance to the unpredictable relationships of act and
consequence than by this confrontation of a father
with his unknown natural son; or to the idea of consequences come home to roost, than by this quiet
youthful figure, studying "deserving" as he prophetically calls it, while he waits upon his elders.

i v

In *King Lear*, then, I believe it is fair to say, the inscrutability of the energies that the human will has
power to release is one of Shakespeare's paramount

interests. By the inevitable laws of drama, this power receives a degree of emphasis in all his plays, especially the tragedies. The difference in *King Lear* is that it is assigned the whole canvas. The crucial option, which elsewhere comes toward the middle of the plot, is here presented at the very outset. Once taken, everything that happens after is made to seem, in some sense, to have been set in motion by it, not excluding Gloucester's recapitulation of it in the subplot. Significantly, too, the act is not one which could have been expected to germinate into such a harvest of disaster (the old King's longing for public testimony of affection seems in itself a harmless folly: it is not an outrage, not a crime, only a foolish whim) any more than Cordelia's death could have been expected to follow from her truthfulness or Gloucester's salvation to be encompassed by a son whom he disowns and seeks to kill.

All this, one is driven to conclude, is part of Shakespeare's point. In the world he creates for Lear, action is cut loose not simply from the ties that normally bind it to prior psychic causes, but from the ties that usually limit it to commensurate effects. The logic of the play is mythic: it abandons verisimilitude to find out truth, like the story of Oedipus; or like the *Rime of the Ancient Mariner*, with which, in fact, it has some interesting affinities. Both works are intensely emblematic. Both treat of crime and punishment and reconciliation in poetic not realistic terms. In both the fall is sudden and unaccountable, the penalty enormous and patently exemplary. The willful act of the mariner in shooting down the albatross has a nightmarish inscrutability like Lear's angry rejection of the daughter he loves best; springs from a similar upsurge of egoistic willfulness; hurls itself against what was until that moment a natural "bond," and shatters the universe. Nor do the analogies end with this. When the mariner shoots the albatross, the dark forces inside him that prompted his deed project themselves and become the landscape, so to speak, in which he suffers his own nature: it is his own alienation, his own wasteland of terror and sterility that he meets. Something very similar takes place in Shakespeare's play. Lear, too, suffers his own nature, encounters his own heath, his own storm, his own nakedness and defenselessness, and by this experience, like the mariner, is made another man.

To some in Shakespeare's audience the scenes on the heath may have brought an additional shock of recognition. It was not simply that they could see there, as we do, a countryside not located in any imaginable England or at any imaginable time but in an eternal moment of human possibility. Nor was it simply that the torrential passion of the old King would come to them trailing long memories of the psychomachia of the morality plays, with Kent, Gloucester, and the Fool playing the parts of characters formerly assigned such names as Mr. Watchful, Mr. Good Will, and Mr. Innocent. What must have struck some of Shakespeare's contemporaries far more forcibly than this was that here a structure they had long associated with pastoral romance, the most popular of their literary and dramatic genres, had been turned topsy-turvy and charged with undreamed of power. In the action of pastoral romances, which is nearly as predictable as the action of an American Western, the protagonist ordinarily moves out in a sweeping arc from the world of everyday, where he has met with problems or experiences that threaten to disintegrate him, to an Arcadian countryside or forest, where nature is fully in sympathy with things human, and there undergoes a learning process that consists in part of discovering his own problem reflected in those he meets. Having confronted his problem in another, having sometimes in the process undergone something like a ritual death and rebirth, he is able to return to the everyday world restored to serenity and often to temporal felicity. The broad characteristics of the pattern may be studied in Sidney, in Montemayor, in Sannazaro, and in such of Shakespeare's own works as *A Midsummer Night's Dream*, *As You Like It*, *A Winter's Tale*, *The Tempest*, and perhaps others.

That Shakespeare has based the ground plan of *King Lear* on a version of this pattern can be seen from a glance at *As You Like It*. In both plays, we have an extruded ruler, and an ugly thunderhead of passion which closes the doors of "nurture" to the more sympathetic members of the *dramatis personae* and impels them to seek "nature." There is a wind which is urged to "Blow, blow" because it is not so biting as ingratitude; a Fool, who knows he has been in a better place, but is loyal. There are rustic primi-

tives, who in *As You Like It* are the comical William
and Audrey, in *King Lear* Tom of Bedlam and the
country people who figure in his mad talk. There are
good and evil brothers, the good brother in both plays
leading an old man—in *King Lear*, his father, in *As
You Like It*, an old servant who has been as a father to
him; and there is a daughter of the extruded ruler,
herself an exile, who is reunited to her father before
the play ends.

Obviously, it is the differences here that count. Yet
even the differences have a surrealistic resemblance.
As You Like It moves from extrusion to magical forests where everyone meets, as in a glass, reflections of
what he is. To the good Duke, the forest discovers

> tongues in trees, books in the running
>   brooks,
> Sermons in stones, and good in everything.

To Orlando, it discovers first a community of "kindness"—that is to say, natural feeling—when he meets
the Duke and his men preparing food and is invited to
partake. Such "kindness" is precisely what he has
vainly sought at home, and what he himself exempli-
fies as he carries Adam on his back and forages sword
in hand to feed him. Soon after this, the forest discovers love to Orlando. To Jaques, by contrast, the forest
brings the stricken deer, abandoned and self-pitying
like himself, whose "sobbing" he accompanies with his

own "weeping." To Rosalind it brings tongues in trees, but not in the same way as to her father: to her the trees speak of love and in rhyme; their "fruit" is Orlando, found by Celia under an oak "like a dropped acorn." Touchstone, as we might expect, unearths in the forest an Audrey; Silvius woos a Phoebe; Celia, who has given up everything to accompany Rosalind, meets with an Oliver, who has also learned by this time to give up. To each visitor the forest brings according to his capacity; and following an exhibition of Rosalind's "magic," which in some respects resembles a ritual death and rebirth (her withdrawal as Ganymede to reappear as Rosalind), all except Jaques leave Arcadia for the world.

King Lear alludes to such patterns but turns them upside down. It moves from extrusion not to pastoral but to the greatest anti-pastoral ever penned. Lear's heath is the spiritual antipodes of the lush romance Arcadias. Nature proves to be indifferent or hostile, not friendly. The figures are not Arcadian, but the wretched fiend-haunted villagers of Edgar's hallucinations. The reflections of his condition that Lear meets are barrenness, tempest, and alienation, the defenseless suffering of his Fool, the madness of a derelict beggar who is "the thing itself." And though a ritual death of sorts occurs at the close of this anti-pastoral, followed much later by a rebirth, all that is thus won is no sooner won than snatched away.

v

I come now to the other dimension of the play on which I wish to comment: the profoundly social character of the world that contains and defines its action. Shakespeare's imagination appears to have been so fully oriented toward a presenting of experience as a web of ties commutual that characterization, language, themes, even the very *mise en scène* are influenced. The play's physical setting, on a "vast and designedly vague terrestrial platform, roofed by a malignant sky," as one critic has described it, proves on close examination to be separable into several distinct landscapes. The prospects sketched out when Lear divides the kingdom are evidently aristocratic, consisting of broad feudal domains "With shadowy forests and with champaigns rich'd." But these fade off in Edgar's speech as he disguises himself to a countryside of "low farms,/Poor pelting villages, sheep-cotes, and mills." This in turn hardens and darkens for the storm scenes into a lonesome heath, where "for many miles about/There's scarce a bush." Conversely, at Dover, we are permitted glimpses of highgrown fields of sustaining corn, together with the weeds and wildflowers in which by now the mad King seems to have decked himself; and of course of the famous imagined cliff, where "half way down/Hangs one that gathers samphire, dreadful trade!" and the fishermen on the beach below "Appear like mice."

The implication of all these settings, it will be no-

ticed, is social. Even on that literally and emblemati-
cally lonesome heath, we are never allowed to forget
the nearby presence of what Mr. Eliot calls in his *Dry
Salvages* "the life of significant soil." Somewhere just
beyond the storm's rim, Shakespeare evokes through
Tom of Bedlam's speeches a timeless community of
farms and farm villages, their nights measured between "curfew" and "the first cock," their beggars
"whipp'd from tithing to tithing," "the green mantle"
of their standing pools broken by the carcasses of "the
old rat and the ditch dog," their white wheat mil-
dewed by "the foul Flibbertigibbet," who also gives
poor rustics "the web and the pin, squinies the eye,
and makes the hairlip." Yet around and within this
primeval community, interpenetrating our consciousness of it at every point, he evokes also a different one,
courtly, sophisticated, decadent. A society of "brothels," "plackets," and "lenders' books." A society
where serving men "proud in heart and mind" wear
gloves in their caps and serve the lust of their mistress's heart; and where, as Lear will say later, the
beadle lusts for the whore he whips, the cozener is
hanged by the usurer, and "Robes and furr'd gowns
hide all."

By such multiple backgrounds and conflations Shakespeare dilates his limited foreground story of a family
quarrel and lodges it in our imagination as a parable of
society of all places and times. The characters too bear
signs of having been shaped with such a parable in
view. As a group they are significantly representative,

bringing before us both ends of a social and political spectrum (King and naked beggar), of a psychic spectrum ("wise" man and fool), of a moral spectrum (beastly behavior and angelic), and even both ends of a vast spectrum of time, showing us a primitive society that is also urbane, an ancient and legendary Britain that is at the same time insistently Elizabethan. Further, as has often been pointed out, most of these characters are unabashed *exempla* of evil and good: "human nature," to quote Bradley, "decomposed into its constituent factors." In Cordelia and Edgar, we have two distinct categories of human virtue, the clairvoyant and the naïve. Cordelia is able to say to her sisters from the start, "I know you what you are"; whereas Edgar, though perhaps he has no compelling reason to suspect a brother who has been out of the country nine years, begins, nevertheless, from a position overcredulous like his father's, and has a "nature . . . so far from doing harms/That he suspects none." The other members of the younger generation offer what appears to be a similarly studied diversification of types. According to one producer of the play, we meet with "heartless intellect" in Edmund, "impure feelings" in Goneril, "unenlightened will" in Cornwall, "powerless morality" in Albany, "unimaginative mediocrity" in Regan. We need not accept these particular descriptions, but they do call attention to a somewhat schematic variety in the play's *dramatis personae*, which the well-known antiphonal characterizations of Lear and Gloucester only enhance. Lear's character, as everyone knows, gives expression primarily to elements in human nature that are intellectual; Gloucester's, primarily to elements that are physical and sensory. Lear, like the soul in Renaissance psychology, initiates and resists. Gloucester, like the body, suffers passively and looks for exits. What Lear finally sees, in his great analysis of society in the mad scene at Dover, is an intellectual vision: his passions, as Lamb said, churn up and disclose to the bottom "that sea, his mind, with all its riches." When Gloucester finally sees, he sees "feelingly," the play tells us; he has no words to unpack his heart; even at death, he evidently says little, but in a kind of dumb pathos, "Twixt two extremes of joy and grief," dies smilingly. The two men's prayers for the helpless show best the measure of their difference. Lear instinctively exclaims, "O I have ta'en too little care of this," and marks it out as the business of men to "show the heavens more just." Gloucester assigns the whole problem to a higher dispensation: "Heavens, deal so still."

Shakespeare sets out this radical polarity of his two protagonists in images both visual and verbal of "leading" and being "led." Lear, his elder daughters assure him, should be "led/By some discretion that discerns his state"; but instead, as Cornwall sardonically remarks when the old King plunges into the storm, he "leads himself." There will come one magnificent moment when he will be led by Cordelia, but the overpowering effect of that moment will arise precisely from the circumstance that we have everywhere else seen and heard him leading himself—repudiating Cordelia, storming out of Goneril's house, rushing away from Gloucester's, scolding the elements on the heath, rejecting the proposed interview with his elder daughters after the battle, brushing imperiously aside those who would divert his attention from Cordelia in the final scene. Contrariwise, we everywhere find Gloucester being led. He is led by the nose by Edmund in the play's early scenes, led by his old servant after his blinding ("my father, poorly led!" Edgar cries), and led finally by his true son, who has become poor Tom, through a world where it no longer surprises him that "madmen lead the blind."

It may be that the mixture of heart-rending homeliness and windswept grandeur in the characterization of Lear himself owes something to the play's concern to exhibit the widest possible range of human potentiality. Lamb found it impossible to reconcile the Lear he saw in the theatre, an old man tottering about the stage with a walking stick, turned out of doors by his daughters on a rainy night, with the apocalyptic figure, cut on the lines of Milton's Satan or some sculpture by Michelangelo, which he took to be the true Lear of Shakespeare's imagination. Yet both Lears are equally in the play, and help, like the antiphonies between Gloucester and Lear, or between the good and bad children, to extend its "anatomy" of mankind.

v i

This concern with society, lightly traced, as we have seen, in the landscape and characterizations, expresses itself strongly in the system of relationships that the play presents. To an extent unparalleled in the other tragedies *King Lear* stresses relations of service and of family—the two relations, as W. H. Auden has reminded us in an arresting essay, from which all human loyalties, and therefore all societies, derive. Family ties, which come about by nature, cannot be dissolved by acts of will: hence the enormity of Lear's action in the opening scene and of his elder daughters' actions later. Service ties, however, being contractual, can be dissolved by acts of will, only the act must be ratified on both sides. Kent, like Sam Weller in *Pickwick*, refusing to dissolve his relation with his master, illustrates the crucial difference between the two types of affiliation. The essentials of the service bond can be restored even though Kent is unrecognized and in disguise. The essentials of the natural bond between Cordelia and Lear, or Edgar and Gloucester, can never be restored apart from mutual recognition and a change of heart.

Ties of service and ties of nature lie closely parallel in King Lear and sometimes merge. It has been argued that one way of interpreting the broad outlines of the story would be to say that the lesson King Lear must learn includes the lesson of true service, which is necessarily part of the lesson of true love. Once Lear has banished true love and true service in the persons of Cordelia and Kent, it is only to be expected that he will have trouble with false service and false love in a variety of forms, including Oswald, his daughters, and his knights, and that he should need, once again, the intercession of true service in the form of the disguised Kent.

Gloucester, too, we are told, has to learn to distinguish true service. At first he veers toward servility. His "I serve you, madam," addressed to Regan, echoes closely on his son's "I shall serve you, sir," addressed to Cornwall, and this is followed by his allowing the castle to be shut against the King. Beginning thus by serving badly, he is badly served in turn by Edmund, and it is only after he becomes a true servant, going to Lear's rescue at the risk of his life, that he himself is truly served, first by his old tenant, and subsequently by Edgar, who it is plain, upholds love and service in the subplot as Kent and Cordelia uphold them in the main plot. Like Kent, and also in disguise, Edgar leads and protects his father. Like Cordelia, he presides over and becomes the instrument of his father's recovery of such happiness as the play allows. And he it is, appropriately enough, who at last destroys both Oswald and Edmund.

The term "service," with its cognates and synonyms, reverberates through the language of *King Lear* like that bell which reminded John Donne we are all parts of a single continent. It is by no means the only highly charged social term to do so. Almost as prominent in the play, and equally pertinent to its sketch of man-in-society, are the other generic terms of social responsibility—"meet," "fit," "proper," "due," "duty," "bond"—and the generic terms of social status, or of social approbation and disapprobation: "gentleman," "knave," "fool," "villain," "rogue," "rascal," "slave," "fellow," and many more. Some of these last, to be sure, are simply vehicles of the contentiousness that crackles in this frantic realm of kings and beggars. But several of them carry in solution searching questions about the nature of human polity which from time to time the action of the play precipitates out, just as it precipitates out the language patterns of sight and blindness, nakedness and clothes into real blindness and real nakedness. What does it mean, for example, to be a gentleman? Is it to be, like Kent, a man of "blood and breeding"; or is it to be, like that "serviceable villain" Oswald, "gentleman" to a Goneril? In the second act, these two very different gentlemen are made to encounter, and though the real gentleman puts the false to rout by power of nature, by power of authority—that great image of authority which makes "the creature run from the cur"—he is ejected in favor of the "super-serviceable finical rogue," whose only true titles, the play tells us, make him "knave, beggar, coward, pandar, and the son and heir of a mongrel bitch." Echoes of the play's continuing debate on this issue may be heard even in the ravings of Edgar and the chatter of the Fool; for "the Prince of Darkness is a gentleman," we are assured by Edgar, with titles of his own—"Modo he's called, and Mahu"; and perhaps all the more for this reason, in the Fool's opinion, "it is a mad yeoman that sees his son a gentleman before him."

Or again, how does a man become a fellow? By being born to menial status, like some of the serving men to whom the term is applied? By losing status altogether, like Kent and Edgar and Lear, to each of whom it is also applied? Or does one become a fellow simply by being man—any man—everyone's fellow by virtue of a shared humanity? During the heath scenes, when Lear, Kent, Edgar, and the Fool become fellows in misery as well as in lack of status, this question too is given a poignant visual statement. Gloucester, coming to relieve Lear, rejects one member of the motley fellowship, his own son Poor Tom: "In, fellow, there into the hovel." But Lear, who has just learned to pray for all such naked fellows, refuses to be separated from his new companion and finally is allowed to "take the fellow" into shelter with him. For as Edgar will ask us to remember in the next scene but one,

the mind much sufferance doth o'erskip,
When grief hath mates, and bearing fellowship.

v i i

Questions like these point ultimately to larger questions, over which the action of the play, like Hamlet's melancholy, "sits on brood." One such has to do with the moral foundations of society: have our distinctions of degree and status, our regulations by law and usage, any moral significance, or are they simply the expedient disguises of a war of all on all, wherein humanity preys on itself (as Albany says) "Like monsters of the deep"? This problem pervades the play, but it is pressed with particular force in the utterances of the mad King on encountering Gloucester in the fields near Dover. Here, as so often in Shakespeare, we encounter an occasion where the barriers between fictive and real are suddenly collapsed, and the Elizabethan audience realized, as we do, that it was listening to an indictment far more relevant to its own social experience than to any this King of ancient Britain could be imagined to have had. The gulf between medieval social ideals and contemporary actualities must have been imposing by Shakespeare's time a significant strain on sensitive minds, the kind of strain that maddens men, as it has in a sense maddened Lear. "The ideal was still Christian," writes Crane Brinton, who has put the matter as pithily as anyone: "still an ideal of unity, peace, security, organization, status; the reality was endemic war, divided authority even at the top, . . . a great scramble for wealth and position." Lear's vision of society in Dover fields is a vision of this gulf. To a limited extent it relates to his own sufferings, but principally to the society for which it was written, and, I would wish to add, to all societies as such. Under the masks of discipline, Lear's speeches imply, in any imaginable society on earth, there will always lurk the lust of the simpering dame, the insolence of the dog in office, the hypocrisy of the usurer who hangs the cozener, the mad injustice of sane men's choices, like Lear's in disowning Cordelia. Institutions are necessary if society is to exist at all; but, as Professor Arthur Sewall has eloquently pointed out, they are not enough. What also is required, if polity is ever to become community, we are shown in the ensuing scenes of mutual humility and compassion between Lear and Cordelia, Edgar and Gloucester.

A second question that the play brings before our imaginations in its social dimension is the problem of human identity. It sees this, in part, as a function of status, and it is certainly not without significance that so many of the play's persons undergo drastic alterations in the "statistical" sphere. Cordelia is deprived of her place in state and family; Kent, of his earldom; Edgar, of his sonship and patrimony; Gloucester, of his title and lands; Lear, of the whole fabric of familiar relations by which he has always known himself to be Lear and through the loss of which he falls into madness. Yet the matter is also presented to us at a deeper level than that of status. When Lear cries out at Goneril's, "This is not Lear. . . . Who is it that can tell me who I am?" or, on the heath, staring at Edgar's nakedness, "Is man no more than this?" we realize that his questionings cast a shadow well beyond the limits of the immediate situation, a shadow that involves the problem of human identity in its ultimate sense, which has lost none of its agonizing ambiguity

with the passage of three centuries. Is man, in fact, no
more than "this"?—a poor bare forked animal in the
wind and rain—or is man a metaphysical conception,
a normative term, which suffers violence whenever
"man's life is cheap as beast's" because the "need" has
been too much "reasoned," whenever "man's work"
(as with Edmund's officer) excludes drawing a cart
or eating dried oats but not the murder of his own
kind?

v i i i

The ultimate question to which all other questions
in *King Lear* point is the question of man's fate—and
here, I believe, we encounter as much of its tragic
theme as may ever be extracted in words. To what
kind of universe, friendly, hostile, or indifferent, does
man's little world relate? By the time he meets
Gloucester on Dover fields, Lear seems to realize that
no certain answer to this question is likely to appear.
He had always been told that he was "everything,"
had supposed that the very thunder would "peace"
at his bidding; but he obviously knows better now.
He has begun to learn patience, and patience, as he
defines it in this scene with Gloucester, is not at all
what he had earlier supposed. He had supposed it
was the capacity to bear up under the outrages that
occur in a corrupt world to oneself; and so he had
cried, when Regan and Goneril joined forces against
him, "You heavens, give me that patience, patience I
need!" Now, with his experience of the storm behind

him, his mind still burning with the lurid vision of a world where "None does offend, none," because all are guilty, he sees further. His subject is not personal suffering in what he now says to Gloucester; his subject is the suffering that is rooted in the very fact of being man, and its best symbol is the birth cry of every infant, as if it knew already it had been born in pain, to suffer pain, to cause pain.

Thou must be patient; we came crying hither:
Thou know'st the first time that we smell the air
We wawl and cry.

Or as George Gascoigne had put it, giving an old sentiment a new turn in his translation of Innocent III's *De Contemptu Mundi:* "We are all borne crying, that we may thereby expresse our misery; for a male childe lately borne pronounceth A" (for Adam) "and a woman childe pronounceth E" (for Eve): "So that they say eyther E or A: as many as discend from Eva. . . . Eche of these soundes is the voyce of a sorowful creature, expressing the greatnesse of his grefe."

Lear's words to Gloucester, I take it, describe this ultimate dimension of patience, in which the play invites us to share at its close. It is the patience to accept the condition of being human in a scheme of things where the thunder will not peace or even begin at our bidding; where nothing can stay the unfolding consequences of a rash act;

>   where the worst is not
> So long as we can say "This is the worst"

—yet where the capacity to grow and ripen is in some mysterious way bound up with the capacity to suffer and endure:

>   Men must endure
> Their going hence, even as their coming hither:
> Ripeness is all.

From this tragic knowledge, Lear later wavers as Gloucester wavers after the battle from what he thought he had learned at Dover Cliff. Lear would need no crumbs of comfort if his sufferings could now be counted on to bring rewards—if, for example, he could pass his declining years in peace and happiness with Cordelia. He wants to believe that this is possible. He has made the choice that he should have made in the beginning. He has allied himself with those who in the world's sense are fools; and he is prepared to accept the alienation from the world that this requires, as the famous passage at the opening of the last scene shows. In this passage he puts aside Goneril and Regan forever; he does not even want to see them. He accepts eagerly the prison which marks his withdrawal from the world's values, for he has his own new values to sustain:

> We two alone will sing like birds i' th' cage:
> When thou dost ask me blessing, I'll kneel down
> And ask of thee forgiveness: so we'll live,

And pray, and sing, and tell old tales, and laugh
At gilded butterflies, and hear poor rogues
Talk of court news; and we'll talk with them too,
Who loses and who wins, who's in, who's out;
And take upon 's the mystery of things
As if we were God's spies.

They will be in the world, but not of it. On this kind of sacrifice, he adds, "the gods themselves throw incense."

But to speak so is to speak from a knowledge that no human experience teaches. If it could end like this, if there were guaranteed rewards like this for making our difficult choices, the play would be a melodrama, and our world very different from what it is. So far as human wisdom goes, the choice of the good must be recognized as its own reward, leading sometimes to alleviation of suffering, as in the case of Gloucester's joy in Edgar, but equally often to more suffering, as in the case of Lear. For Lear, like many another, has to make the difficult choice only to lose the fruits of it. Not in his own death—as Kent says, "he hates him/ That would upon the rack of this tough world/ Stretch him out longer"—but in Cordelia's. Cordelia, our highest choice, is what we always want the gods to guarantee. But this the gods will not consent to. Hence when Albany exclaims, at Edmund's confession that he has ordered Cordelia's death, "The gods defend her," the gods' answer to that is, as Bradley pointed out long ago, "Re-enter Lear, with Cordelia dead in his arms."

In the last speech, the full implications of the human condition evidently come home to Lear. He has made his choice, and there will be no reward. Again and again, in his repetitions, he seems to be trying to drive this final tragic fact into his human consciousness, where it never wants to stick:

> No, no, no life!
> Why should a dog, a horse, a rat have life
> And thou no breath at all? Thou'lt come no more,
> Never, never, never, never, never!

He tries to hold this painful vision unflinchingly before his consciousness, but the strain, considering everything else he has been through, is too great: consciousness itself starts to give way: "Pray you, undo this button: thank you, Sir." And with it the vision gives way too: he cannot sustain it; he dies, reviving in his heart the belief that Cordelia lives: "Look on her, look, her lips,/Look, there look there!"

Professor O. J. Campbell says at this point: "Only to earthbound intelligence is Lear pathetically deceived in thinking Cordelia alive. Those familiar with the pattern of the morality plays will realize that Lear has found in her unselfish love the one companion who is willing to go with him through Death up to the throne of the Everlasting Judge." My own view is that the matter is less simple. Though there is much of the morality play in *King Lear*, I think it is not used toward a morality thesis, but, as I have tried to suggest in these pages, toward building a deeply metaphysical metaphor or myth, about the human condition, the state of man, in which the last of many ambiguities is the inscrutability of his relation to the enigmatic universe by which he is enclosed. To realize his humanity, to become anything more than a well-clothed animal, he has to act as if there were a moral order behind the thunder, and yet he must make this choice, if he makes it, knowing that it will never necessarily be vindicated—not at any rate, by the light of this world. He may find, like Gloucester, that his Edgar lives; he may find, like Lear, that his Cordelia dies. There can be no certainty or there could be no merit. All we have to go on, as Mr. Eliot puts it in his *Four Quartets*, is hints and guesses—hints followed by guesses.

In such a world, the play shows us with a remorseless logic, we must seek the meaning of our human fate not in what becomes of us but in what we become. Death is miscellaneous and commonplace; it is life whose quality may be noble and distinctive. Suffering we recoil from, but it is a greater thing to suffer than to lack the feelings and the virtues that make it possible to suffer. Cordelia, we may choose to say, accomplishes nothing, but it is better to have been Cordelia than to have been her sisters. When we come crying hither, we bring with us the badge of our mortal misery; but it is also the badge of the vulnerabilities that give us access to whatever grandeur we achieve.